Girl in High Heels

Girl in High Heels

Intimate confessions of a London stripper

Ellouise Moore

EBURY
PRESS

1 3 5 7 9 10 8 6 4 2

Published in 2008 by Ebury Press, an imprint of Ebury Publishing
A Random House Group Company

Copyright © Ellouise Moore 2008

Ellouise Moore has asserted her right to be identified as the
author of this Work in accordance with the Copyright, Designs
and Patents Act 1988

The Random House Group Limited Reg. No. 954009

Addresses for companies within the Random House Group can be
found at www.randomhouse.co.uk

A CIP catalogue record for this book is available from the
British Library

The Random House Group Limited supports The Forest Stewardship
Council (FSC), the leading international forest certification
organisation. All our titles that are printed on Greenpeace approved
FSC certified paper carry the FSC logo. Our paper procurement
policy can be found at www.rbooks.co.uk/environment

Printed in the UK by CPI Cox & Wyman, Reading, RG1 8EX

ISBN 9780091927172

To buy books by your favourite authors and register for offers visit
www.rbooks.co.uk

To David; friend, brother, uncle and better father figure than I could ever wish for. Thanks for being a constant reminder of the good men in the world.

Contents

Acknowledgements

Special thanks to my excellent agent, Rowan Lawton, for putting up with my over-anxious, panicky moments.

Lena Semaan, for the constant help at all hours and giving me confidence in my ability to do this. (And for coming to a lesbian strip bar with me!)

Charlotte Cole, Rachel Rayner and everyone in the team at Ebury Press.

Thanks to all the friends I met while dancing, especially Tamara and Melissa; for always sticking up for me, standing by me and making things that little bit more bearable. And everyone else, you know who you are.

And finally, to all the stalkers, enemies and oddballs. Thanks for the salacious content you inadvertently provided. Without you it just wouldn't have been possible!

Disclaimer

This book is a work of non-fiction based on the experiences and recollections of the author. Names of people, places and the detail of events have been changed to protect the privacy of others.

Prologue

I looked over at the VIP area of Stringfellows – or Strings, as we called it. It was the place where the big money usually congregated. There was a large group of men there, all of whom seemed to be smothered in dancers, but this particular man sat alone. He didn't look very happy. In fact I think he would have been more animated in a bank queue. I watched as he turned away girl after girl and continued to stare listlessly into his brandy glass. The reason I kept watching was that he seemed to be the one spending all the money on everyone else's behalf. I decided to approach him and start talking. It was always a bit of a gamble when you did that since you never knew whether you were on to some serious money or just wasting time. I had a good feeling about this and recently I was finding my hunches were usually right.

We began talking and he quickly gathered I was something of a newbie and not the hardened, money-chasing bitch that many guys dread. He was American, an older man, very well-educated and genuine. It turned out he was taking clients out for the night and being in the club was something he was clearly doing for them: he found it highly uncomfortable. I spent the rest of the night chatting to him about various things – travel, books, films – and he seemed to take a liking to me. Not in a sleazy way. He thought I was different from the other girls and really shouldn't be in the job. I'd heard all that before: a lot of men think like that and want to save you. We call it 'knight in shining armour syndrome'.

Still, he was nice. And he was just about to get nicer. When it was time for his party to leave he reached into his pocket and pulled out a huge wad of notes. I didn't look at how much he'd given me until he'd left. It was nearly four grand! I'd never held so much money in my life. It was easily my most profitable night so far. Although I regularly made good money at Strings, nights like this were pretty special.

There was another time when I was offered almost twice that amount by an Arab prince. But that's another story.

Chapter 1

∽

Girl in an oversized G-string

My name is Ellouise, sometimes called Ellie and, occasionally, Ali, but you can call me Ellouise. I was a stripper, for want of a better word, for around nine years. I've done a lot but there are a lot of things I didn't or wouldn't do – those were the things I saw and heard. I'm now 28 and I've done the hardest thing for a stripper to do: I quit. I suppose I'd better tell you how I ended up here.

I'd phoned Stringfellows and asked for an audition. A girl I knew had suggested it when she found out I was broke. If you've ever wondered how someone decides to become a stripper it doesn't involve major decision-making, just a desperate need for money. I'd just come out of a destructive relationship; the culmination of three hard years having had to move out of home after

3

my parents' separation (more of which later). I'd been scrabbling around earning bits of money since I was 16 and I was fed up. I wanted to earn real money and be able to look after myself properly.

That Tuesday afternoon I nervously dialled the number, half hoping that nobody would answer.

'Stringfellows. Can I help you?' It was a woman's voice.

'Uh, hello,' I stammered, 'I'd like to audition for a – um – job as a – um – dancer.' OK, I meant stripper. But I wasn't sure what I was supposed to call the job.

'Auditions are held Tuesday evenings at 7pm. Come through the back entrance and tell them why you're here. You'll need to bring a cocktail dress, heels and a G-string. Don't be late.'

Before I'd got the chance to thank her, let alone ask what the hell a cocktail dress was, the line went dead.

That was reasonably painless. I put the phone down, relieved until I realised that today was Tuesday. God, I had to get my act together and audition in a few hours. Where on earth was I going to find a cocktail dress? And a G-string? I know it might sound strange now but G-strings weren't that popular back in the late 1990s. Sure, you could get them in underwear departments and speciality shops but they weren't the sort of thing you'd find in your local high street. And that's where I was, with hardly any money to spend. I also had to make sure I had enough to get the train from Kent to London for the audition. In a blind panic I went down the local market and, sure enough, there was a tacky stall selling the kind of knickers I wouldn't even use to wipe the floor with now. They were horrible and only seemed to come in hideous colours like flesh and salmon pink. Not knowing anything about size, I picked up a G-string and bought it for 50 pence. The rest of my outfit would have to be put together from my severely limited selection of clothing: basically I had one dress and one pair of heels.

The dress was a floral-printed summery confection that looked like something you'd wear to tea with your granny. It stopped below my knees, which didn't seem sexy. (I honestly had no idea what was sexy at the time; but I just knew this wasn't.) I took a pair of scissors from the kitchen drawer and cut a random chunk from the hem. The shoes would have to be my only pair of heels, a four-year-old pair of ugly black wedges with an ankle strap. Looking back, I was like the Super Saver budget version of a lap-dancer.

I took the train and arrived in Covent Garden with about thirty minutes to kill. I wasn't too far from Strings so I wandered into a shoe shop, looking at what I would later realise were the plastic stripper shoes that all the girls wore. There was a branch of Pret A Manger almost directly across the street from the club where I knew I could disappear undetected into the toilets and hide for a while. While I was there I applied my makeup – if you can call it that. I had 99 pence worth of brown eye shadow which I daubed across my eyelids with my finger, since I was not big on makeup and had never thought to buy a brush. I followed this with a sweep of equally cheap mascara. I still had ages before my audition and couldn't think of anything else to do so I just stood in the toilet brushing my hair to kill time. Everyone raves about my hair now but back then it just seemed limp and mousey blonde. I hadn't ever had it coloured and it'd been a long time since I had it cut. I actually reminded myself of my religious education teacher at school, who'd been a new age hippie. It was not a good look. Although I vaguely knew I was attractive and had a good figure, I was like a lot of girls in that I lacked both confidence and the knowledge to make the most of my looks, let alone how to present myself for an audition like this.

Finally it was time to head down the road to Stringfellows. I managed to find the back door, took a deep breath and opened it. Suddenly what I was about to do hit me, but it wasn't nerves: it was excitement. I can only explain it in terms of the way my life had been going up till then, which was far from ideal. I felt that I had absolutely nothing to lose by going for this audition and it might just be the break I needed; the start of something better.

That feeling of euphoria changed almost as soon as I entered the dimly lit club. Any confidence and sense of anticipation deserted me and I was left instead with a horrible, sick feeling in the bottom of my stomach. Looking around at the plush furnishings, opulent chandeliers and enormous, brightly lit stages where the girls danced was pretty overwhelming and I found myself breaking into a sweat. What was I getting myself into? It suddenly dawned on me that I knew nothing about this world. I'd never seen strippers and had no idea what the job really involved. As I was led downstairs past the ornate, gold baroque mirrors and the decadent red velvet curtains, I began to realise just how far out of my depth I really was. I was an ordinary little girl in a grown-up world.

It got even worse when I saw the Stringfellows girls. If I'd wanted to be in a place that reminded me how insignificant I was then I couldn't have chosen better. These were the girls who already worked at the club and I was going to have to audition in front of them. I'm not small (5' 7") but they all seemed to be tipping six feet and the Amazonian effect was enhanced by gravity-defying breasts, sexy tight dresses, stiletto heels and diamonds. Plus they all had that tan of women who'd been sunning themselves for a month in the Caribbean. At the time I didn't realise that a lot of this was an illusion, a fantasy they created with money and a lot of effort.

My first instinct was to run: it's always been my way and even years later, it would always be my first resort when I was afraid, insecure or angry. Instead I forced myself to follow the directions to the toilets where we hopefuls had been told to get changed. There were four other girls in there with me. With their bleached blonde hair, heavy, expertly applied makeup, clear plastic stilettos (the shoes I'd seen in the shop earlier) and neon stripper dresses that left little to the imagination, they all appeared to be experienced dancers. Looking at them at that moment it didn't matter whether or not they were beautiful: they just looked right.

I, on the other hand, felt like the runt of the litter with my badly applied eye shadow and mascara, my chiffon dress and my clumpy black heels. I'd not been on holiday since I was ten years old, had never used a sunbed and had no idea that fake tan even existed. The saddest thing of all was the G-string I'd brought with me. I was very slim and it was so big it came up really high, over my belly button. I looked like a child who'd raided her mother's closet and got it drastically wrong.

All changed and ready to go, I took a deep breath and prepared to leave the safety of the toilets, where girls were doing elaborate, mind-boggling stretches and layering on the glitter.

Tentatively, I walked out to the floor and towards the huge main stage. It was shaped like a catwalk and surrounded by mirrors. What on earth was I doing in this place? I was so desperately out of my league. But I was also desperate for a job.

'Who wants to go first?' asked a man who I gathered was one of the managers.

I'd already figured it was a clever move to go last, so I could watch what the seasoned strippers did. I hoped to pick up a few tips and use them in my dance.

Maybe that wasn't the best idea after all. These girls knew what to do with a pole almost as if they'd been born clinging to one. They started spinning around on the pole, hanging upside down and removing their clothes, all while doing the splits in mid-air! I almost found it too much to watch. Now it was my turn. I remember standing up and walking towards the stage and then it seemed to be over. I'm not sure whether they felt sorry for me and so ended my turn early, or whether anxiety had hijacked my brain and I was so spaced out by fear I no longer had any concept of time. I can't even remember what song I danced to.

Anyhow, I think I managed a pretty good approximation of a wiggle and managed to take off my dress while hanging nervously on to the pole for dear life, which was about all I could do with it. The good news was that I didn't trip over my dress or get it caught on my shoes, and somehow the feeling of nausea stayed away long enough for me to do what I had to.

Once I'd finished I was told to get changed and then to come back to the floor and wait with the others. The manager came over and went down the line asking all the girls the same questions.

'Where have you danced before?'

'How long have you been dancing?'

'How old are you?'

'Are you dancing anywhere now?'

He didn't ask me anything. Not one question. When he'd finished with the girl next to me, he turned and went back. Was I so bad – terrible even – that he didn't want to waste his time on me? I was thinking about this as he went back along the line and dismissed the first three girls. They were really good dancers – which probably meant I didn't have a hope. Strings probably gets hundreds of calls a week from girls who want to audition, which means they can pick and choose.

'Sorry girls, we don't have space for you right now. Good luck.'

The rejected girls just got up and left. Only I and one other girl remained. She wasn't as experienced as the ones who'd been sent away, but I thought she was pretty good. The manager was talking about shifts, club rules and trial nights. I just sat there confused. He obviously wasn't talking to me. Maybe he'd forgotten to send me away? Maybe he'd told me to leave but I was panicking so much and hadn't heard him? I wasn't sure if I should just sit and wait for him to stop so I could leave without interrupting him.

'Trial nights are Thursdays. You need to be here at 7pm.'

It was the manager. It sounded like he was talking to me. He was!

'I think it might be a good idea for you to speak to some of the other girls before you start your shift. You'll also need to talk to the House Mum. She's the person who looks after the girls behind the scenes and she'll tell you what you need to do.'

I sat there dumbstruck. At some point before he walked off, I managed to ask him about the details for Thursday, just so I could make sure I'd heard right. It was true: I was in. I got the hell out of there as fast as possible. I was petrified that he'd call me back and say he'd changed his mind. I stepped out into the mild night air of Covent Garden. In two days I'd start work as a dancer.

For those who haven't heard of Stringfellows, it's probably the most high-profile lap-dancing club in London or even the UK. I suppose you could describe the interior decoration as 'bordello luxe' with both floors decked out in red velvet and leopard print. On the top floor, which is the street level where the punters enter, there's an enormous stage with two smaller podiums on either side. The way it works is that the best girls are showcased on the main stage while those who are not so glamorous or popular yet are hidden away on one of the podiums. Needless to say, I began on one of the podiums – where most girls do their apprenticeship. There's also a large restaurant upstairs decked out in crushed velvet and with gilt chairs covered in leopard print. A chrome and glass staircase takes you to the basement floor which is basically just a really big space with tables and a catwalk-style stage in the middle. Sitting at one of these tables requires you to buy a bottle of champagne which could cost upwards of £150 a pop (excuse the pun). The more you spend the nearer you get to the stage and, of course, to the girls. Around the edges of the club are the VIP areas. This is where the real money sits. There are mirrors and red velvet everywhere – the walls, ceilings, carpets, chairs and curtains are covered in it. It's all rather '80s but in a funny way it sort of works.

Girl in an oversized G-string

Strings is a big club. At any one time there are around seventy skimpily clad, spray-tanned, bleached blonde, overly made-up girls working there. OK, that doesn't apply to absolutely everyone but there are many who fit that description exactly. The dancers range in age from eighteen to around forty, although if you asked this latter group they'd be quick to say they were actually thirty-ish or even younger. When I started in the mid-'90s, most of the girls were English. Peter (Stringfellow) liked English girls. Also, while it's probably the most prestigious club in London, attracting a high proportion of celebrities and very wealthy clients, you can earn more money elsewhere. This tends to be offputting to the foreign girls who are usually out to make as much money as possible, no matter what the conditions.

The daily routine would see everyone coming into work, converging on the club at about 7pm. Seventy girls would cram into the tiniest changing room and bustle around, jostling each other in a bid to obtain a fraction of mirror space. There really wasn't much room for a girl to get glamorous in: there was a wall of lockers on one side, a wall of mirrors on the other and a hanging rail in the middle. Very soon a thick blanket of perfumed fog would fill the air, a mixture of just about every aerosol beauty and hair product on the market. The place was teeming with hairdryers, hair straighteners, heated rollers, tubs, bottles and tubes of makeup, moisturiser, fake tan, deodorant, perfume, nail polish, hairspray, fake eyelashes, diamantes, hair removal cream, teeth whitening preparations, coloured contact lenses, fake hair and that all-important glitter.

Somewhere around was the House Mum, who in this case I'll call Gemma. Gemma's job was to be helpful; she was supposed to do things like find you a needle and thread if your costume needed a repair and generally maintain order. She actually did very little and I found her rather unhelpful and bitchy. She received fifteen pounds per shift from each of us (I'm not sure if it all went to her or if only some of it did). There was also a hairdresser and a makeup artist, both of whom we avoided like the plague since the former would burn half your hair off and the latter would make you up as if you were about to appear in a horror film, something I was to discover for myself very soon.

For all of these reasons and many more, I took to changing in the toilet. Once the process of beautification was over, the troop of girls would take their surgically enhanced bodies to the floor and wait for the punters to slowly trickle in. This was the worst part of the evening. You had to be ready for opening at seven-thirty even though nobody is going to come in that early. The girls would sit around and drink and smoke (remember you could smoke indoors then!). In some respects that explains why a large proportion of dancers have problems with drink, though there are many other reasons for that.

Chapter 2

∞

You just stand there and wiggle

I was feeling pretty good as I got on the train for my first night of work. My bag was packed with the same dress and shoes I'd worn to the audition. I'd figured that since I got the job in them, I must have looked OK. The insecurity that had plagued me at the audition two days earlier had gone, and I was grinning from ear to ear.

As soon as I arrived at the back door of the club, just like the first time, everything changed. Walking into Strings can be intimidating and I suddenly felt like a little girl again. The Egyptian security guard, who was very sweet, figured out that I wasn't feeling too good.

'Hello dear, how are you?'

'Um, OK, thank you.'

'It's your first night, isn't it?'

'Yes …'

'Don't worry, everything will be all right. It's a good place to work. Good luck.'

'Thank you.'

'And if you ever need to talk to somebody, I'm always here.'

I wanted to chat to him a bit longer, if only to delay entering the dark corridors of the club. I waved goodbye to him in his little cubicle as I headed down the stairs to the main floor, where I proceeded to wander around aimlessly, unsure whether to tell someone I'd arrived or even who that person should be. At one point I attempted to ask a couple of girls for help but I'd only just opened my mouth when they pushed past me without so much as a glance. Someone eventually pointed me in the direction of the changing rooms where I soon found myself underneath very strong lights surrounded by semi-naked girls jostling each other, screaming greetings across the room and making the sort of racket only a group of girls can make.

I started to get changed into my dress and G-string – I'd splashed out on some new knickers that actually fitted. I knew I was supposed to find the House Mum but had no idea who she was. One of the girls indicated the far corner of the changing room so, doing my best to navigate between bags and bodies, I headed over

17

there. The House Mum was easy to spot. She was an older woman, probably in her early forties, and there was a definite air of authority about her. I approached her and began to speak but she spoke over me to somebody else. Not wanting to be rude or do the wrong thing I stood there until she'd finished and then tried to introduce myself again. She looked hard at me before writing down my name. Without saying a word she turned, dug out a battered pair of clear plastic high heels and told me to put them on. Wow, I was going to wear proper stripper's shoes! Not only that but I was going to have my makeup done. Of course at this point I didn't know I'd never want the makeup artist to come near me again but on my first night it felt glamorous to sit in a chair and have someone do my face – until I saw the results.

When I looked in the mirror I wanted to cry. The makeup artist had plastered my face with foundation which was at least five shades away from my own skin, then layered ghastly orange blusher on top of that. She'd drawn sharp black eyebrows on top of my unkempt blonde ones and painted my eyes in black, highlighted with white glitter. I was horrified: gone was my fair skin and freckles and in its place was this transvestite-like creature! I didn't know what else to do so I thanked her as sincerely as I could, took my prized stripper shoes and followed another girl who'd been told to give me 'the basics'.

'This is the main stage and upstairs is the show stage – the front one – and the podiums – at the back. Now remember the names 'cause when the DJ calls your name, he'll say the name of the stage he wants you on and you have about three minutes to get your arse up there. The rest of your time you just go around and hustle.'

I wasn't sure exactly what she meant: 'hustle' was completely new terminology to me but I mumbled 'OK' and she was gone.

I'm the third girl on stage, I've had about four glasses of wine, there's maybe forty guys watching and it's just dawned on me what I am about to do. All I can do is stand here and sweat. Oh shit! I'm wearing – actually I'm wobbling in – the stripper shoes which have four-inch heels. In ten minutes or so I'll be on but right now my stomach is churning so fast I'm running back and forth to the loo. What happens if I get like this on stage? God, it doesn't bear thinking about. OK, I'll try not to think about it. What shall I think about instead? I'll hum. Isn't that what people do? They hum to regulate their breathing. It's not working. Lucky I'm in a mild alcohol-induced haze because otherwise there'd be no way I'd go up there. Is this really a good idea? Too late. I'm on.

Up until that point I'd filled in time trying to introduce my feet to the stripper shoes – with limited success as I could hardly walk in them. I'd been in the toilets attempting to rub off or at least subdue the heavy makeup (I could barely move my face, the foundation was so heavy) and then I'd sat in a corner watching everything going on around me. The barman had given me a glass of wine. In fact I think my nervousness was so apparent that the sympathy vote was flooding in from every direction, as that glass of wine was followed by three more from a customer (that or he just got off on the fact that I was barely legal and petrified) so I was pretty pissed by the time it was my turn to perform.

I actually went on stage about five times that first Thursday night. At Strings you're on a 'stage rota'. In other words you get called to the stage and you move your arse pronto. This can be anything from five to ten times a night. The payoff comes when customers who've observed your prowess on stage call you over for a private dance. As soon as I finished my second stage show (I'd fled to the bathroom after my first) a guy called me over to dance for him. I'd been so focused on the stage up until now that I really had no idea what the hell to do. I stood about three feet away from the guy, barely spoke to him and did a slightly rushed striptease, hardly moving. I hurriedly pulled my clothes on again, took the money and ran.

I'd done my first lap-dance, even though I was a long way from his lap and it was far from dancing. I spent the next half-hour walking round studying what the other girls were doing – and realising how bad my dance was. The next time I came off stage, someone asked me to dance for him and I was prepared. I carefully executed a routine I'd copied from another girl and from that moment on, dancing was never a problem. I'd danced competitively as a child and knew I had rhythm: it was just a case of getting everything working together in this environment. Once you know the technique it's the easiest, most natural thing in the world. I was already dancing like a pro – professional dancer, that is!

There was a ritual at Strings that I – and all the other girls – hated. At midnight you had what they called 'The Parade of Angels'. This would consist of all the girls lining up like sheep waiting to be dipped and then walking on stage in order of merit. Peter Stringfellow, who owned the club, would decide the order. Yeah, I know: very nice. There was an even worse 'tradition' though: at regular intervals during the course of the night the DJ would play Motley Crue's song, 'Girls, Girls, Girls', and you'd have to stop what you were doing, find a customer and do them a free dance. It was fine if you were already with a customer but otherwise it felt pretty desperate even though everyone did it. I'd try and hide in the loos, but if you got caught sneaking off you were fined. I hated it so much. One minute you're in the changing room trying to cover up a spot on your bum and the next you're running out and jumping around in front of some guy, looking totally pissed off and bored. It was really stupid.

The night would come to a close at approximately 3.30am when the girls would stampede into the changing room to get into the money queue, except for the ones who were totally wasted or still trying to get money out of customers. During the course of the night, customers would pay you in cash or vouchers; vouchers could be bought on credit card from a booth in the club and carried a 20 per cent charge. You'd collect your vouchers – also known as 'heavenly money' – and hand them in to the House Mum at the end of the night. Did I mention you had to pay to work here? For each shift you gave the club £75 plus the £15 you paid to the House Mum.

I made £160 profit that evening and went home almost tearfully happy. Barely a couple of months later that amount would leave me feeling seriously unimpressed. But for now, I was happy. I'd passed the first test. I sobered up, scraped off as much of the makeup as tissues would allow and walked to Charing Cross station to sit and wait for the first train of the morning at 6am. I was in a dream world, still slightly tipsy but elated, and the two-hour wait for the train could have been five minutes. It was the start of my new life.

After that I was given more shifts. Over the next few months I found my feet – both on and off the stage – and started earning good money. You'll be pleased to know that I was still wearing the same dodgy outfit I'd auditioned in even though a brand-new pair of stripper shoes had been added to the ensemble. I still hadn't worked out how to apply makeup or do my hair – all I knew was that I wouldn't be visiting the in-house makeup artist again. I was still very rough around the edges and not quite the finished article. But all that would come in time.

Chapter 3

I am whatever I say I am

Anyone entering a lap-dancing club and expecting it to resemble some sort of Roman orgy would be disappointed. Don't be fooled by girls walking around in skimpy dresses; the atmosphere here is calculated and controlled. There'll usually be a general bar area where girls who aren't dancing for anyone will be sitting around drinking and having conversations among themselves in their cliques. Should you listen in you'll find them talking about the most mundane things possible: periods, phone bills, acne, running late for the hairdresser's – the sort of stuff any group of girls might talk about over a drink. Then after a few glasses of wine the conversation changes to bitching, gossip, customer stories, body parts and their sexploits.

'You know my customer Tim, the small guy with the bald head?'

'Yes.'

'He's so fucked. Seems he's been having an affair with his secretary and now she's pregnant. Only problem is his wife's pregnant as well.'

'God, men are fucking idiots sometimes, aren't they?'

I really enjoyed these gossip sessions. I felt like I belonged. Since I wasn't yet part of any crowd at Strings, this part of the evening allowed me to join in. Mostly my first few months were spent sitting on the periphery – literally – rather like the new kid at school. I'd listen to them talking and wouldn't offer anything myself: I wasn't that confident yet. I still felt like the little girl listening to her older sisters talking about things she'd never done. But I wasn't stressed about it. I just took it as part of my learning experience. I didn't spend too much time worrying that I wasn't part of the cool set: I had far too much to absorb. That didn't stop me from sitting there wide-eyed trying not to let my mouth drop open when they talked about their lives!

There were always a few guys around as well: the men who worked there. More than likely the bartender would be male and, aside from the security guys who stood next to the velvet rope outside, there would also be a couple of them inside, just keeping an eye on things (and usually eyeing up the girls as well) and making sure the patrons didn't get out of hand. The last thing a club wants is trouble, so ensuring things run smoothly and quietly is important. Early on in the evening with the club barely full there's not a lot of atmosphere; that only materialises when the punters start rolling in, which is usually after ten o' clock. You might have a few guys turn up before then; they'll usually be regulars looking for a dance from their favourite girl and, often, to spend the rest of the evening talking to her.

Most clubs like you to wear evening dresses until a certain time, usually until the punters started crowding in, and then the girls let loose with costumes. Some of the costumes at Strings were pretty spectacular, as much for their sheer ghastliness as anything else. My particular favourite, as much for its comedic value as anything else, was the G-string with long straps which went up all the way over your shoulders instead of your hips. (These have since been christened the Borat Bikini after the wonderful Ali G character, who sported something similar.) These came in an assortment of fluorescent colours. Sometimes they were trimmed with diamantes, tassels or fake fur. Also in Lycra and available in a variety of lurid colours were jumpsuits: these came with holes in the sides – or anywhere else, for that matter. In case you didn't feel warm and sweaty enough, they also came in PVC.

For some reason American flag bikinis were very popular. There was also, predictably, a wide array of fancy dress. On any one night there might be nurses, maids, schoolgirls, teachers, military personnel, cowgirls, cheerleaders, bunnies, police officers, angels, devils, pirates, Mrs Santa, gangsters, Wonder Woman, flight attendants, a Roman goddess, Tarzan's Jane, genies, German beer maids, and my all-time favourite, the nun. The first time I saw it all I thought it was pretty mad but I soon realised why the girls did it: wearing costume allowed the girls to distance themselves from the customer and indulge in harmless role play. The customers love the costumes and the playful games: they don't want you to be the girl they've got at home, no matter how gorgeous she is. This was all part of being a performer and that's what I was.

It only took me a couple of months to figure out what worked for me. First of all I realised that men responded to me because, unlike a lot of the girls, I looked natural. I hadn't had any surgical enhancements, didn't wear fake tan and, after that awful first night, went easy on the makeup. So it seemed appropriate that I should sell myself on the fresh, sweet and innocent look, especially as there were so few girls who had it. That meant natural makeup with visible freckles and a look that said, 'I'm eighteen and I've just started here'. Pulling this together wasn't that difficult. It was simply a case of sticking to costumes that were pretty and girly rather than overtly sexy. I loved wearing babydoll dresses and lacy underwear with frills so I didn't have to do too much that was out of character.

My G-strings were usually white as were my hold-up stockings or over-the-knee socks. I knew my act was the best way for me to make as much money as I could. I can understand how it might sound cringe-worthy, even disgusting, to some people, but my job was all about acting and I was simply playing a part. I kept it as classy as possible: I never wore a school uniform or, as I've seen some girls do, wear big white children's cotton panties. I tried to look more virgin bride than underage, but then it's often a fine line!

As the years went on I tended to choose outfits I liked, rather than dressing just for the punters. Being more womanly and worldly than when I started meant I could pull off sexier outfits, and I felt good in them. What really opened my eyes was a visit to Ann Summers, a high street chain selling, among other things, sexy lingerie. Ann Summers is really popular with strippers and it's where I first discovered sexy underwear. My first purchase of many was a pink baby-doll dress with frilly bra cups and sweet knickers that tied at the sides. I loved it so much that when I brought it home I wore it for five hours! I knew I looked good and it made me feel really confident about myself. I stuck to pastels and later on, opted for all black.

I also began to style myself on my favourite pin-ups, like Jayne Mansfield and Sophia Loren in *The Millionairess* as well as my favourite Bond girl, Ursula Andress. I used to re-enact the Bond girl bikini scene that Andress was famous for and the guys really loved it. With my long wavy hair and tall, athletic frame, they told me I looked just like her. What girl wouldn't want to hear that? While a lot of girls would change their costumes and their look each month, I stuck with what I knew best and my 'Hollywood Idol' look worked for the majority of my career. I just never felt right dressed as a cowgirl or a nurse.

You're probably wondering about the dancing itself. Sure, there are some girls who really put on a show: I have one friend – and she's still dancing – who can do the most amazing acrobatics. One minute she'll be upside down on the pole fully clothed, holding on only with her legs, and the next minute she'll be upright, wearing nothing but her G-string and a smile. In the intervening minutes she's managed to manoeuvre herself around the pole and remove her clothes! The interesting thing about her was that she liked doing it for herself; she's one of those girls who saw what she did as a theatrical art form

– as it can be – and liked to put on a show as much for her sense of personal achievement as for the punters. Part of it was the challenge of pushing yourself to extremes, always learning new moves then executing them perfectly while still looking sexy and working with the music. A performance worthy of a top circus performer is something to be proud of and the girls who do these plan every last detail – music, moves and costumes – so that every performance is different from the last.

When I first saw these girls I was so intimidated. Despite the fact that I'd trained as a dancer at school and had good coordination, my speciality had been Irish dancing, which didn't require the kind of strength and agility these girls had, not to mention the fitness. I know that some gyms now try to teach the basics of the pole for fitness but the girls who do it well just looked utterly comfortable with it. From the beginning I knew that I wasn't going to be that sort of dancer. First of all I didn't have the upper body strength required – you need some serious muscle for those upside-down manoeuvres – and secondly I realised that I could do just as well without becoming a master of the pole. Not to mention that I'm an absolute klutz, so doing pole work is just asking for trouble.

My own approach was much more subdued and involved sexy, swaying moves while playing with my clothes in a suggestive manner. I can't say I planned it either. After watching the girls in the first week I realised it was all about the tease: you'd play with the silk strap of your camisole, pulling it down over your shoulder and then pulling it up again, each time just showing a hint of nipple, and so on. Eventually you'd pull the strap down, and then you'd do things to keep it all very suggestive, like covering your breasts with your hands then slowly removing them, sliding them down your body to reveal your bosom. Every girl has her signature move. Mine was my hair flick: when you're on stage you bend forward, letting your hair slip over your face, then slowly flick it back as if what you're doing is the most natural thing in the world. If it's a private dance you flick your hair so it gently brushes the customer's cheek. Every move I made was done gently, almost in slow motion.

Although a private dance was only four minutes long, there were times I'd stand there wondering how much longer I could keep fiddling with my clothes. Eventually I'd just remove them and get down to my G-string. Often I got bored and stopped before the four minutes were up and the men were none the wiser – everyone does it, usually over half of the time. Some girls were known for their ability to get away with doing two-minute dances. Back then at Strings it was only about stripping down to your G-string. (Now it's the same in most places: you take everything off.)

My night would usually consist of having a glass of wine or three and waiting for the customers to roll in. When they did turn up, the club filled very quickly, so there was always plenty of work to go around. But you had to hustle for it. You'd go on stage a number of times each night and the idea was to scan the crowd to see who was interested; i.e., who you could target for a dance when you got off the stage. The trick was to make eye contact with men so that when you came off stage you had 'buyers' who were ready to part with their money. Making eye contact with men made them feel special and they'd think you were looking at them because you obviously fancied them. Believe me, that's the way most guys think, whether they're attractive or not. In many ways this whole business is built on a fantasy that everyone plays their part in, consciously or not.

When you come off stage the guys with whom you've made eye contact will usually ask you for a private dance. If a guy doesn't do it straight away, a clever girl will file him away in her brain and return to him later in the night. She'll also know who not to bother with. If a guy is more interested in his brandy than you, you don't take it personally. You just don't waste time hustling him. When you're up on stage you also have a good vantage point to watch the guys who aren't buying. Spotting them will save you a lot of time later.

A girl's ability to read her audience is very important in selecting targets for a private dance. There are all sorts of lines strippers will use on customers depending on how they've read the guy. Some girls are really up front. They'll jump off the stage, grab a man and say, 'Come on, let's have a dance.'

Others are even more overt and will simply say, 'I have the most amazing breasts, let me show them to you' or 'I've got a freckle right there next to my nipple, do you want to see it?' And of course they do.

Me? Well I took the sweet, sexy route, batted my eyelashes and said something like, 'Oh I'm so embarrassed, I didn't mean to stare at you but you remind me of someone I dated.'

Sometimes I'd really lay it on thick and pretend I was shy and unsure of myself. Men loved it because it made them feel very masculine. Saying something like, 'I'm sorry to interrupt you but I'm new here and this is all a bit awkward for me. Can I join you for a while until I get my nerve back?' would have them absolutely eating out of my hand. Many of them were only too willing to have me sit with them. The thought that they were rescuing me was too good to pass up. I became pretty adept at figuring out what men wanted to hear. A lot of men, even intelligent ones, don't want a smart girl (not in a strip club anyway). It was often in a girl's interests to act dumb, even if she wasn't.

Usually you made your money dance by dance, with the customer putting the money in your garter. At £10 for about four minutes it would add up as long as you kept working. Sometimes you'd hit the jackpot and get a 'sit-down'. This is basically the customer paying you an agreed sum to sit with him in the VIP area for half an hour or more. You might do the odd dance for him, but mainly it's just some chat and a lot of flattery and flirting. Some men get turned off if you talk about money, so you really have to trust your intuition and hope that when you do spend time sitting with someone it'll pay off. You can average two hundred pounds an hour but it's not unusual for girls to be given thousands. What is even better is having a regular wealthy customer whose visits can lead to a constant money tap: gifts, airline tickets and even cars. The sky is truly the limit.

A girl might say something like, 'I'd love to stay but I have to keep working,' the implication behind her hesitation being that she has to earn money. This is the cue for a man to say, 'No, sit with me; I'll look after you.' What you don't want is to end up with only two hundred pounds for two hours of a sit-down when you could have been dancing for far more than that and possibly meeting a more lucrative sit-down in the process. A good stripper has to be able to factor in all these things and make quick decisions in order to make good money.

The first few months at Strings were a big period of adjustment in every respect. I was learning about the practical nature of stripping as well as the emotional side. I was working long hours so was spending a lot of time alone. For now, it suited me – after my parents separated, life had been pretty turbulent and it was good to focus on something that I was good at and introduce some stability into my life. Most of the girls I'd known at school went to university. I'd wanted to go but my parents' circumstances meant I couldn't afford to, so I lost touch with almost everyone except for two girls. When I started dancing they had negative opinions about stripping so I found it easier to see less of them rather than wondering if I'd have to argue the toss every time. On the rare occasions we did get together, I knew we were already miles apart. Dancing had made me very confident in a way they couldn't understand. It wasn't something you could explain to them and eventually I accepted that's just the way life went. In any case there were so many people around to distract me, some of whom would eventually become friends.

After four or five months at Strings I was starting to feel pretty pleased with myself. I felt comfortable in the environment and confident in my ability to handle the work. With each passing month I began to increase the amount of money I earned. I could now afford to move into a flat that was closer to the station – still a short bus ride away – so I could get into London from Kent in forty-five minutes. It was then that I decided to tell Mum what I was doing. She was fine with it. I never thought she wouldn't be: she'd brought me up to be very strong and disciplined and I think she had even more faith in my ability to conduct myself than I did – which is quite a lot. She asked some questions – mainly out of curiosity – but she had absolutely no doubt, as I did, that I knew what I was doing.

That didn't mean I didn't find it overwhelming: this surreal world of naked women, velvet and leopard skin. I'd work long hours, go to bed about 7.30am, get up about 3pm and then I'd need to have a bath and get myself ready all over again. By now I was building up a regular clientele. A girl's regulars might come in daily, weekly or monthly, but these guys turn up specifically to see a certain girl. They come for different reasons. Some want to see you undress. Others want someone to talk to because they're lonely. Most regulars don't hang around once they realise you won't go to dinner with them and therefore definitely won't sleep with them. So they move on to the next girl. By that point you're usually so fed up with them pestering you to go out with them that you're more than happy to pass them on to someone else. Some are an absolute pain in the arse: there was one who was young and reasonable looking but he was so arrogant I could barely stand him. Of course I knew my livelihood depended on showing exactly the opposite so I had to play it carefully. For weeks he'd beg me to fuck him and I'd repeatedly reject him in as many gentle ways as I could.

'Go on, you know you want to.' (I didn't.)

'But you're a customer so I'd lose my job.'

'Aw, come on, it can't hurt. Don't you like me?'

'Oh I *really* like you, but I just think it'd be weird meeting you here and everything. If only we had met somewhere else'.

He was persistent. 'Give me your number, let me call you.'

Hmm. This was getting difficult. I was running out of excuses. I ended up telling him I had no mobile phone and I never gave out my landline: nine years ago that was still a respectable excuse! The next day he came in with a present for me – a mobile phone. I was all out of excuses so I had no choice but to blatantly reject him. I kept the phone though!

While I didn't realise it at the start, my youthful, relatively 'un-stripper-like' looks gave me a certain naïve air that made me very popular with customers who liked young women. Don't get me wrong; they didn't all have paedophiliac tendencies. Lots of guys just didn't want a girl who knew too much or looked like she knew too much, which is not unlike real life when you think about it! They were indulging a fantasy. Using my youth as a money earner never troubled me until one day my eyes were rudely opened to another, less innocent side of the strip scene. I was mid-dance for a guy who'd become a regular when he leaned forward, obviously very aroused, and whispered: 'You look just like my niece, she's 12.'

I never danced for him again.

Chapter 4

It's 2am. Do you know where your husband is?

Working at Strings brought with it the possibility of coming into contact with innumerable wealthy men. I hate to admit it now but back then it was pretty exciting knowing that the club attracted these types. The aura of wealth is hugely seductive and being around it impressed me at first. It was a side of life I'd never seen. Landing one of these guys was a pretty big deal. I remember the first time a customer bought me a hugely expensive bottle of Cristal champagne: I was so excited but did my best to pretend that yes, I was grateful, but I was used to it too. He probably knew I wasn't but he didn't let on.

While many of the rich guys were businessmen, entre-preneurs and bankers you'd also get a fair few celebrities popping in. Television stars, actors, musicians and models: Peter knew *everybody* and they often came to sit with him. In the beginning it was hard not to look when you saw them but after a couple of months, I figured they were just people and watching them get drunk and behave badly brought that home to me pretty quickly.

On one occasion we had a very famous singer in, someone who is now solo but used to be in an early-1990s boy band. He was a regular at the club and a good mate of Peter's. I was dancing for another customer when he suddenly came reeling across the floor – drunk – and smashed into me. He actually knocked me to the floor mid-dance so my customer had to help me up. Oblivious to the fact that he'd spoilt things not just for me but for my customer as well he carried on walking with no apology or offer of assistance. That really pissed me off. I didn't care how famous someone was: there was never any call for rudeness. Still, within minutes he had at least ten girls draped all over him. Later on that night, he called me over for a dance and I politely refused. All the other girls were shocked. I reckon I must be one of very few girls to turn down this tattooed Lothario and reading about him now, he's still pretty much the same.

Then there was a very handsome footballer, who drunkenly called me over for a dance. Mid-dance he pulled me aggressively into his lap. I jumped up and slapped him and then walked off and left him to it. The next day I had a visit from 'his people' with a formal apology, kindly asking me not to go to the press (which is something I would never do anyway). I reassured them I wouldn't do anything of the kind as he actually seemed like a really nice guy who had just got drunk and got carried away. There were countless other celebrities who would go home with girls but I've always avoided being a meaningless shag to someone who won't remember my name in the morning. It's just not my thing.

If I'm being truly honest, I didn't want my job to be anything but work: I wanted it to stay separate from my life. Flirting never came naturally to me but I learned to act the part so the idea that I would take this outside the club with a customer was a totally alien one. While knowing that men wanted me to dance for them boosted my confidence, I didn't have any interest in knowing them beyond that. After the very difficult period following my parents' separation I wanted financial security. It meant everything to me and I knew that to achieve it would require me to stay focused and not get distracted by the social side of stripping. If it wasn't for the money I wouldn't have been stripping because all the adoration in the world wouldn't have made a difference. While emotional security is infinitely more important than anything money can buy, the fact is that I wasn't ready to give myself emotionally to anyone at this point and if I was going to, it wouldn't be to a customer. The line between work and personal life for me was easy to see.

Making money meant doing your homework and learning a few tricks. I found there were lots of ploys a stripper can use, ranging from outright deception and scamming to using her brain. It all depends on your personal morals, or lack of them. Some girls will always make false promises to guys. They'll have them spending money all night long in the false hope that they'll meet up afterwards. Frequently a girl will make plans to meet a guy in their hotel, a local bar or for dinner the next day, all the while making them stay hour after hour, with each hour costing hundreds of pounds. I know girls who have had guys doing sit-downs for four or five hours while promising to go back to their hotels. Of course they don't turn up. I've even heard of girls taking half of the money for the 'night' – so the guy has shelled out £800 in the VIP area and given her another £1,000 as a down-payment for sex that night – and then not showing. There have been cases where one or two of the 'jilted' guys have complained the next day, but most guys are too embarrassed at their own behaviour to do so.

While I didn't go this far, I lied to guys; you have to. They don't come in to hear the truth. If you told a guy 'I hate this job: you're a fat, sweaty loser and all of the guys that come in here are idiots', you probably wouldn't get a sit-down (even though there's always the one guy who's into degradation!). Or if you told a guy 'I'm in a wonderful loving relationship, adore my boyfriend and if you weren't paying me I would never talk to you', he would run a mile and you'd have no customers. So to an extent, lying is an integral and necessary part of the job. And I didn't see it as lying so much as playing a character.

One of the easiest and most common tricks is to get a guy drunk. It may sound bad, but that's what they come in for. No man wants to drink alone but most of all they want to get you drunk as they think that will enable them to have their way with you. Most girls are wise to that, so have a couple of tricks up their sleeve. Usually this means having a prior arrangement with the barman so all the cocktails they serve you are non-alcoholic – even though the guy is buying you alcoholic cocktails. A lot of men like you to drink champagne with them – it makes them feel extravagant and powerful.

Any girl drinking champagne all night is not going to be able to dance, so if your objective is to make money you have to be a bit clever. Basically you have to get rid of it, and that means tipping it on the floor or into a plant when he's not looking. You do this while you're constantly telling him to top you up and pushing him to keep up with you. This way he'll drink twice as much and you'll drink nothing. A drunk guy is much more likely to spend money than a sober one, and much easier to manipulate.

A more subtle strategy is paying attention to a man's clothes. A guy's suit will tell you whether he's new money or whether he has wealth and unflashy good taste. Watches and shoes are also good clues as to whether your potential customer is likely to pay off. A cheap watch, or no watch, usually says no money. Perhaps he's just started earning and hasn't explored the watch route yet or perhaps he simply thinks they are unimportant. Either way, he's not the guy you want to dance for. The men who wear the big-name bling – the Franck Muller, Breitling or Rolex – usually signal new wealth: either they haven't been on big money long and have just started with watches or they have limited style and taste and have got stuck at the hurdle of 'big name equals big price tag' and are often poseurs. The trouble with these men is they're often more mouth than money. Finally you have the men who wear the understated watch with a leather strap. It may be vintage or new, a Jaeger LeCoultre or IWC, but you can be sure that even though it's subtle, it cost a bomb. These are the guys with money and style; they don't just earn big money, they usually own the company.

I love a man in a good suit and working at Strings taught me how to spot them. A Savile Row suit stands out and so does its wearer. There is no belt since the suit has been tailor made for him and where the bottom of the trouser meets the shoe there is only one gentle fold, indicating perfect length. The lapels, stitching and lining are all crafted with utmost attention to detail. The shirt he's wearing will be made to order as well so that the sleeves are at exactly the right point between the bones of the wrist and where the thumb joins the rest of the hand. He may or may not be wearing cufflinks: this is down to personal preference. This man understands clothes and what suits him. He knows what he wants. And it's usually the best.

The next step down are the guys who buy the big money off-the-rack suit, e.g., Dolce & Gabbana, Canali, Brioni, Armani, but ignore the fact that it needs to be altered for fit. Then you have the lowest rung: what I call the phone salesman suit. It's slightly shiny, there are two or three folds at the bottom of their trouser, and the jacket is square-cut, making it look like a box and the wearer like a robot. The thing about cheap suits is not that they're cheap but that they usually don't fit – unless you're the sort of person who looks good in anything.

Too many men let their suits down with bad shoes. Shoes can make a huge statement. What you're looking for are good leather shoes that have been cared for and are not scuffed or worn. They will be lace up and will have an elegant leather sole. A man wearing an expensive brown or tan leather shoe is a man with both confidence and money. I've known girls to be able to size up a guy's wallet by his tie. I didn't get to that point but always found that a discreet Hermès tie is always a good sign or even better, no tie at all (then you know he's already relaxed).

A man's clothes also tell you what kind of girl he might like. An established, wealthy older type is likely to go for a girl he perceives as educated. For him I'd be 'at uni and just working the odd shift to keep on top of my student debts'. Actually when I wasn't working I spent a fair bit of time keeping on top of political affairs and learning about art, literature and architecture so I could converse with the most cultured of guys. To be honest I'm a self-confessed nerd so I actually loved this part of the job. The guys with the flash watches and designer suits usually liked the stereotypical dumb stripper. If they started talking about their work in hedge funds and you were smart you'd say something like, 'So do you work in gardening or something then?' Guys loved comments like that: it made them feel they were so far above me and their painfully delicate egos needed that. If you showed these men you had a brain you'd disappoint them.

If you're not getting clues from a guy's outfit, you can usually tell from the first twenty seconds of conversation. If they start hitting on you straight away, maybe complimenting you on your bottom or your breasts, you know you've got some horny bloke who wants an equally horny girl so you lay it on thick. You flirt outrageously, and act like he's the sexiest guy you've ever seen. If he's shy then humour's a good way to warm things up, as is acting like you're also shy and have just started. That way he instantly feels an attachment to you. If he's slightly depressed or talking about family/work problems he needs your sympathetic ear, lots of nods and some wise words. He could also do with getting a load of alcohol inside him to help him forget his problems.

It might sound like we spent a lot of our time lying to the guys to get money out of them. But you have to remember that most of the guys were lying to us to get us into bed. We were just so much better at it than they were! But the stuff they came out with was amusing – at first, anyway.

It's unbelievable just how many men are model

agents, casting directors, footballers, pilots, celebrity managers or work in hedge funds. Then there are the ones who say they are friends with someone famous in the hope that you'll sleep with them in order to meet their friend. That particular ploy will go something like, 'Me and Jude ... oh sorry, I meant Jude Law. We were out together the other day ...'

Then there is a whole box of general lies you hear so often you wonder if there's a little book aimed at desperate and unimaginative men.

For example, 'My Chelsea house is being refurbished so I have to spend a lot of time at my pad in the south of France.'

Or, 'My ex-girlfriend was a stripper actually ...'

And, 'You should come and holiday on my yacht sometime.'

And even, 'I used to be a model/stripper/porn star in my heyday.'

Married men who try not to be married are hysterical.

'Married? Me? No, I'm looking for someone lovely who can fly around the world with me – as I have to work all over the world – and while I'm in the office they can just amuse themselves shopping or something. Or someone who doesn't mind being left in my house in Knightsbridge while I'm off working all of the time ...'

Of course you can clearly see the indentation of their

wedding ring and they probably haven't had a stamp in their passport for a long time.

You have to remember that men come into clubs like Strings for loads of different reasons. Their appearance in a strip club is often symptomatic of something that they're either looking for or need to express. Most guys fall into one of the following categories:

The men who want to save you

They want to help you and save you from the big bad world of stripping. They'll happily fall for the 'I'm a poor student' or 'I've just started' because they want to believe it. They tend to be quite nice guys who have families, or are recently divorced but dote on their kids. They are relatively regular and will only have one girl they talk to. They tend not to have dances, never try to fuck you or even ask you out for dinner. They generally want to help you/rescue you.

These customers are few and far between but catching one is a major bonus. Keeping them is very much a case of keeping up the act and constantly showing you appreciate their concern and need them (every guy likes to feel needed) – every man needs his ego flattered but for these guys it comes with gratitude. They don't come in much or stick around for long, but can be very generous

49

considering you don't have to dance for them. On the other hand, talking about your fictional university course for two hours can be hard work in itself.

One girl at Strings was given £20,000 on the premise that she would quit stripping. The guy thought she was 'so much better' than that and wanted to pay for her to go to college and start a new life. She left Strings straight away and within two weeks started working at another club, £20,000 richer. I know so many girls who say they're only stripping to save up for a new car or to pay school fees. One girl's story was that she only did it to put her mum through rehab. The guys would come through with the goods. If you're lucky enough to get what we call a major payoff you have no choice but to leave or the guy might chase you up and it might be more hassle than it's worth. I'd like to think if it happened to me I would have turned it down. I'm not sanctimonious – I just know that everything has a price.

The men who want to marry you

They fall in love with you and honestly believe you are their girlfriend. They tell everyone, including other customers and girls, that you are in a relationship, and are totally deluded. They turn up for most of your shifts and will often leave work early to see you before you get busy. They are good to start with, but after a while you just want to get rid of them. It nearly always ends up disastrously, usually with them realising you're not actually their girlfriend and will never go out with them. The danger is that they could become your stalker.

This happens more than you think. One girl I know has been proposed to twice. Both times the guys have been long-term regulars (for over six months) and believed there was more to their relationship than stripper–punter. This is just an extreme version of a 'save me'. The guy wants to marry you to give you a better life. To be fair there are girls who do marry customers; in 2006 alone, I knew three. A lot of girls want to be 'kept' by a rich man and make it their goal to find one. More often than not they just disappear and turn up months later married. They won't strip again.

The men who want to fuck you

This may be where every man would like to go, but these guys don't beat about the bush. They don't want to wine and dine you or buy you gifts; all they can think about is their hotel that night. You get a lot of young, relatively attractive guys with a penchant for fucking strippers, who come to a club with the aim of not going home alone. They'll lay on the charm, tell you they're actors, footballers or pilots and that they have two grams of coke back at their place. Sadly this works all too often, especially the line about the coke. They have dance after dance and if they're getting nowhere with one girl, work the room until there's a glimmer of hope. These are usually the demanding guys who like a certain thing, i.e., watching a girl dance for a girl, shaking your bum a lot, dancing barefoot etc. If these guys do end up leaving alone you can bet they're off to see a prostitute.

'What would it cost me to sleep with you tonight?'

'I'm not for sale.'

'Of course you are, you're a stripper, you must have a price – £500 … £700 …'

'Honey, I'm priceless and even if I weren't, you couldn't afford me.'

And then we have the guy who's 'in the biz'. Usually the guys who peddle these lines are older.

'God, you're amazing, I work in movie casting and I'm working on this Brit flick that has a part for a sexy temptress, you'd be perfect. I've got a few people "in the biz" coming to mine later, why don't you come over. I could definitely see you as a big actress or something.'

'Nah, I like what I'm doing, thanks.'

And of course we have the guys who claim to be editors of 'lads' magazines'.

'I'm the editor of *Loaded/FHM*, let's hook up later on

as I would love to get you in for a photoshoot, you'd be great in the magazine.'

'*Loaded* must have a lot of editors as you're the third one I've met tonight.'

The men who stalk you

Thankfully, stalkers don't happen often. They can be anything from guys not taking kindly to rejection, to full-on obsessives who follow you home and threaten you. They're often the guys who fantasise about being your boyfriend but it can also be someone you've never spoken to or have only met once or twice. These are the ones to be scared of.

The men who want to be your friend

Sometimes you get these delightful older guys who become friends with all of the girls. Then you get the guys who pay you just to talk because they're lonely. It's incredibly sad that their life has come to this but it's no different to seeing a therapist, just a hell of a lot dearer. I always attracted these guys, partly because I didn't look threatening but also because I could hold a conversation about most things. Sometimes they just wanted to talk about the news or sound you out about their love lives, so you could tell them where they were going wrong, e.g., why they can't get a girlfriend. They might also want to hold hands and cuddle you.

I had one punter who would come in every month, and chat with me for two hours at a time. He was really boring. Frankly it was excruciating, having to talk about nothing for two hours. On the other hand he never wanted a dance, never hit on me and never grumbled about paying me. A customer told me that I was his best friend. It made me really sad that someone I knew nothing about and had little regard for thought I was his best friend, but it happens.

You get guys coming in regularly who have no particular favourites but are friends with all the girls. They are the loveliest, most harmless guys. They're not perverted in any way and are usually the biggest characters of all. These guys always make me wonder as they have such big personalities and kind hearts. Are they spending so much time getting away from bad home situations or just their own loneliness? I don't know, but I suspect the answer is somewhere between the two.

The men who want to be alone

They come in three, four times a week, speak to no one, make half a pint last three hours and spend as little as possible. They might be voyeurs but I also think they like the idea of being able to hide away in this alternative world. They don't speak or acknowledge anyone and don't like to be spoken to.

There's one guy who would come in to a club I worked at in later years. He would never speak to anyone but would sit there all day watching. If you tried to say hi or acknowledge him, he'd squirm. I found him scary: he couldn't communicate normally and was the type of guy you imagined you'd see on the news one day in relation to some horrible crime. He had spray-on hair that would stick to his forehead in summer and it was so hard not to laugh but you wouldn't dare do it to his face. He'd come in every day, spend as little money as possible and just watch everyone.

The power-trip men

The lowest of the low. They come in, degrade you, insult you, shout, swear and call you names. At work they haven't quite made it or they're struggling with female bosses and come in to exact their revenge. They're arseholes. They'll see a pretty girl and immediately decided she's 'up herself'. It's happened to me. They'll be rude to you and when you don't respond they laugh at you, call you a whore and ask why you can't get a real job. They may even go as far as spitting in your face, slapping, punching or kicking you. They're also the guys who grope. Frankly they're the scum that ruin it for the rest of the guys. Their gratification comes from arguments and making a girl cry rather than seeing her strip. There will always be girls in the changing room crying – I did it – because of these power-hungry but cowardly and inadequate men.

Uncomfortable men

They're probably out with a group of workmates or on a stag or some big night and they'd rather be hit in the face with a wet fish than be in the club. They talk about work, blush, stare at the carpet hoping it will swallow them up and are the first out of the door. Again, these are few and far between but they stand out since they're doing their best not to look at the scantily clad girls. Guys will always buy their most uncomfortable friend a dance. Of course they really don't want it but you have to do it as you've been paid. It's awkward on both sides as you don't want to dance for a guy who doesn't want you, but you can do a really crappy dance and just chat and have a laugh while moving around a bit and not really taking your clothes off. He feels like he got off easily and wasn't subjected to a hardcore strip and you earned money for nothing.

The gay guys

They haven't come out at work yet and have come in the club with their colleagues. They try desperately to act like the macho guy who's getting turned on by girls. It's always incredibly amusing from a girl's point of view because you know they're gay. I had a gay customer for a while: he never admitted he was gay, would come in with his two workmates and always have one dance with me. It was patently obvious he was gay but if I asked him he'd say he had a girlfriend.

The fetish guys

Thankfully they don't come in too frequently but they're quite often into young-looking girls – which often meant me, especially when I started. They make awful requests, bringing in white cotton schoolgirl panties and socks, asking you to wear them, wanting you to call them 'Daddy' or 'Uncle'. It's truly revolting and you do your best to keep as far away from these people as possible. You also have the foot fetish guys. They ask you to dance barefoot and touch your feet while you do. There was even one guy who'd bring his wife's designer shoes in and ask the girls to dance in them for him: he'd pay extra for the girls to rub them on their bodies. Some guys ask to put their fingers between your toes, smell your feet, taste them or buy your shoes. I have sold my shoes – that was easy to do! Another thing guys like to do is wear women's tights or lace panties under their suits. They get off on someone else knowing, so mid-dance they might say 'I'm wearing satin French knickers' or 'I'm wearing fishnet tights'. I would just reply, 'Oh, how nice for you'. The weirdest thing I had was a guy asking to buy a lock of my hair, which I refused. While the fetish guys are generally creepy and to be avoided they're a constant source of gossip and giggles in the changing rooms.

Regular guys

Yes, they exist! Normal customers, that is: simple run-of-the-mill horny men who have a few dances with a couple of different girls and drink a fair bit with a group of mates on a night out. Not overly rude, not overly friendly. Fine.

Ladettes

Strip clubs are not an exclusively male-only environment; you do get the odd woman. Sometimes a guy will bring a 'girlfriend' in who is obviously a hooker. I've never quite worked out the reasoning for this except that maybe he's trying to get her all heated up first, but since she's a professional she knows her job! My absolute favourite is the office girl who comes in with a group of guys. You see them desperately trying to fit in with the lads. They'll start out by being absolute bitches, looking the strippers up and down like we're worthless shit and loudly calling us 'tramps', among other things.

'Fucking whore'; 'Look at the arse on that'; 'They're fake'. You hear it all.

By the end of the night they're pissed, their shoes are off and they've snogged at least three of the guys in the group including their boss. Their makeup will be smeared over their face and they have no idea what's going on. More than likely they'll end up in someone's bed and regret it the next day. Who's the tramp now?

After what I've said about the need for a stripper to understand men you'd think most strippers would be wise about blokes. But they're not. Amazingly, a fair few girls 'keep' their boyfriends, who seem to be permanently between jobs. This is more evident with Russian and Eastern European girls as their partners apparently find it 'too hard' to find work. Since the girls are earning such a large amount of money, the need to get a job becomes less urgent. The thing about this that surprises me is that the partner is happy to live off the girl's earnings, and hasn't even thought of working so that the girl doesn't have to strip or even work so hard. Isn't love wonderful?

Chapter 5

❧

A charming devil and his angels

There are some things, that if you explain them to people, they will never comprehend. I will quote an acquaintance of mine, a drug dealer. I once asked him why he did what he did. He replied, 'It's what I'm good at; I don't know anything else and I've discovered it gives me a huge adrenalin rush. Some people skydive or bungee jump but this is my excitement.' I don't want you to confuse this with moral justification: he could have been talking about his job as a crane driver. As it happens he wasn't.

I realised I understood exactly what he meant. I'd been working at Strings for several months now and was totally immersed in it: it was my life. Just being part of the environment was a buzz and I loved being on the stage dancing. The hours were long and it was bloody hard work but I liked working there. At first the only friends I had at the club were the other staff: the Egyptian guy, Amir, who helped me on my first day; Suzie the toilet attendant and a young guy called Dee who worked the bar. These were people I could relate to and felt comfortable being around. On the whole I was happier chatting with them than swapping plastic surgery tips with the girls. They all had their cliques and tended to stick to them, so breaking into a group was pretty hard. It's not dissimilar to most other jobs really: you're an outsider until they accept you.

I'm not someone who walks into a room and has to be the centre of attention. I tend to hang back rather than project myself immediately. I don't mind not being noticed by everyone; it makes it easier to blend in. For me those early months were about observing and there was certainly a lot to look at. If you were casting a Hollywood movie about strippers you couldn't have written better characters.

Take the girl I'll call Charlene (remember I'm using no one's real name, 'stripper name' or otherwise). She was a thirtysomething with an orange tan and a hell of a lot of liposuction behind her. She was one of the Strings 'in crowd', a hardened dancer who earned a lot of money but who also first opened my eyes to everything I didn't want to be. She spent an awful lot of time kissing the arse of anyone she thought could help her, which usually meant Peter and the club's managers. She'd tell anyone who was prepared to listen that a former customer of the club set her up in a flat in High Street Kensington and paid all her bills. Whenever her 'benefactor' came round, her boyfriend would have to go out. I remember him coming in once and it made me shudder: he was a creepy little man and much older. It was revolting.

Next was crazy and sex-mad Marina. Whether you were male or female she didn't care, she'd be all over you. She was always drunk and feeling people up. She gave a constant commentary of her conquests and sexual peccadilloes, some of which surprised even the most worldly girls. She went on holiday with Peter and his girlfriend on his yacht – you can only imagine how much that boat was rocking! They put pictures of their holiday on the website and in Strings magazine so it was no big secret and just added to Peter's illustrious reputation. Her red hair, piercings and brash manner were all part of the package but she was harmless and friendly. I believe she ended up doing hardcore porn – double penetration. You could kind of see that one coming!

Lizzy was Peter's girlfriend for most of the time I was there. She was quite plain but had a great body and was very sweet. She would come to work like any normal stripper, get dressed in her costume but then sit with Peter all night, which slightly defeated the point. He started her off on a singing career but it didn't go too well. They dated for a few years and he apparently bought her a new MG. Peter looked after his girl-friends.

Every strip club needs a Pamela Anderson clone and ours was apparently an official one, who actually did lookalike work. She had the hair, nose, lips, boobs and even the barbed-wire tattoo so that she could replicate Pammie. She was a prime example of a girl who has no life other than stripping or modelling – she lived in a dream world. Her name was, of course, Pamela.

Anjella was a much older girl who told everyone she was 28 but I would easily add ten years to that. She was a nice girl, very approachable and kind. OK, so she was a cokehead and I was later told she was a hooker, but she was still nice. One day she just disap-peared and a few months later I saw her in Covent Garden getting out of a Bentley with a richer, older customer, who turned out to be her husband. She was noticeably pregnant.

Julianne was one of the older girls as well and was dating or married to one of the managers, Roger, a guy in his early sixties. She was scarily thin and pale and never worked. Instead she just sat in the restaurant looking incredibly miserable. I never saw the point of her coming in, as she never earned money and was clearly unhappy.

Bobbi was an absolute liar. She lied about everything from her plastic surgery (she'd had loads but swore she hadn't) to her rich boyfriends. She claimed to be a model who'd made it big in America, but nobody had heard of her. She told some people her boyfriend was a millionaire music producer while also saying he was a top American modelling agent. Perhaps when people tell so many lies they lose their grip on reality and start actually believing it. Some girls are so unhappy with themselves they just lie to make themselves more interesting and likeable.

Jessica didn't need to do any of that. She was absolutely beautiful, very quiet and softly spoken. She was easily one of the most beautiful girls there, with a perfect body to boot. When I first started, I was completely in awe of her. She kept herself to herself, worked hard and earned a lot of money. She was always immaculately presented and perfect, very classy and refined.

As you might expect, girls don't use their own names at work. This lends itself to a wide range of stage names: Bambi, Star, Angel, Brandy, Peaches, Champagne,

Honey, Raven, Candy, Lolly, Porsche, Mercedes, Harley, Emerald, Sapphire, Pixie, Pebbles, Heaven, Summer, Storm, Autumn, Montana, Sydney, for starters. Then you had your slightly less imaginative girls, who went for Paris, Brittney, Sienna, Kylie, Pamela – you can see where I'm going.

It's not just for show, either; there are safety and privacy aspects to consider. If someone shouts 'Ellouise' in the street I know not to turn round as it's probably a customer. This allows me to screen out people. Another reason is that it gives you a degree of separation: when you're a stripper you're acting, playing a part, whether it's a poor student trying to pay off her debts or a horny seductress who totally fancies the guy she is dancing for. When you put your costume on and start playing the part of Ellouise, Brittney, Sugar or whoever, it's a great way to separate what you're doing from reality. For me that separation was essential but it wasn't for all the girls. There are many for whom stripping is their only reality. I wanted my reality to be so much more. I wanted security, friends and hopefully a relationship.

I'd met a new friend called Tamara (not her real name either!) and we instantly clicked in a way that you do only a few times in your life. Tamara is small, dark and cute and I'm tall, fair and leggy so perhaps we liked each other's physical opposite. But mostly we just found it easy to chat, laugh and joke and I was relaxed with her in a way I wasn't with the other girls. Tamara and I were to work together at other places and go through some tough times but to this day we're still friends. She's a real artiste on the pole – something I'm not. She has a touch of the burlesque about her and can execute the most amazing moves while being cute and sexy at the same time. Even when I go to watch her now I'm still amazed at her moves – as is everyone else in the audience.

I'd been working at Strings for about a year – an amazingly quick year – and decided a move to London was now a necessity. I needed some normality in my life and mainly my sleeping patterns. Working every night and going to sleep at 7am every morning was playing havoc with my life. So I moved to North London, to a quiet, safe area. The flat was on the top floor of a two-storey building, had new carpets, a lovely bathroom with a bath, and a nice sunny kitchen. I was in heaven. I moved in my furniture, painted the bedroom and bought new lights and curtains. I would go to sleep in peace and quiet knowing I was in control of my life for the very first time. I bought a big TV, new clothes and a beautiful sofa; my first new possessions since everything I'd had up till then was mostly second-hand or given to me by my mum. I could afford to get a cab home from work so there was no waiting at the train station. I was getting a good night's sleep – and actually going to sleep in the dark. This made me feel more relaxed about things and I could go out again and maybe even date.

That sounded good in theory but combining dancing with dating wasn't easy. First of all it had taken me several months to get used to my new life; simply keeping the late hours was an adjustment and it was hard to see where I'd find the time or the energy to fit in a social life. Stripping was my first real job – before that all I'd had were part-time jobs – so I took it very seriously. At the same time I enjoyed the work and the club so the date would have to be pretty good and he'd have to fit in! About seven months after starting at Strings I met a lovely guy in a club. I'd gone there with some girls from work; we often went out afterwards to hear some music, have some drinks and unwind. It started off well but it didn't take long before he started moaning that I wasn't spending enough time with him and cared more about working (true). When I moved to London I think he saw it as a cue for us to spend more time together but my schedule stayed the same – we were seeing each other once a week and the rest of the time I was absolutely knackered.

He began to hint that it would be good if he stayed at my place more often so he could see me. We had dated for nearly a year but I had no interest in this happening either now or later on. I didn't want it or need it. It takes a lot for me to want to spend all my time with someone: he would truly have to be something special. So we split up. When I broke it off with him, I sat in the bath and cried my eyes out. It wasn't that I had any regrets, but it was the first time that I'd let anyone down, let alone broken their heart. He was a lovely guy but I wasn't the right kind of girl for him. I was enjoying my life too much. I was revelling in my new-found stardom at Strings and lapping up the glamour with the other girls. So, single again and with all of my stripper acquaintances, I would go out and have fun.

I learned a lot about life and people inside the club. I watched and understood how the older girls worked the crowd, how they hustled customers and how they played the managers off and bitched between each other. I learned a lot about the customers, why they were there, what made them tick and what made them open their wallets. Meanwhile I'd built up a regular following of clients and was doing well, so much so that I soon became a favourite of Peter Stringfellow himself. Peter is a fixture on the London scene, a great self-publicist and the guy credited with pioneering the whole lap-dancing thing in London. And he knows everybody: pop singers, politicians, you name it.

Those of you who've seen pictures of him in the press are probably visualising his blond mullet hairstyle and penchant for leopard skin and leather and thinking, 'he's a bit of a sleaze'. In truth he wasn't like that at all. He didn't try it on with the girls, as a lot of people seem to think. He's very well-mannered and a complete gentleman. Sure, lots of the girls threw themselves at him. And while he dated young women I don't think that's any different from a lot of men. In a sense he personified the lifestyle that a lot of his customers wanted to live – and he still does. For that reason I think his public persona was probably very well thought out; the guy is a smart businessman and understands how people think. He's very astute about his market and knows exactly how to create the sort of environment that keeps men coming back. He may seem laid-back but he's always on the ball and he never misses a thing.

When Peter liked you, your life changed. Instead of hustling the floor for work, you'd be invited to join him at his table, where he sat in a leopard-skin-covered gold throne. Sitting at Peter's table was quite a big deal because his guests were usually fabulously wealthy, famous, or both. That fact alone pretty much guaranteed you some seriously good money for the night. On top of that you got to drink fine champagne and were very well looked after. This is where I eventually made friends with some of the other girls. Like me they were his favourites and while all the other girls did their best to catch his eye, he had little time for them. On the other hand his favourites were invited to dine with him and his guests, which made all the other girls jealous. This is exactly where you wanted to be at Strings.

Make no mistake, to be one of Peter's 'Angels' was a pretty big deal. He made it even more of a big deal by introducing you to people in the most complimentary and lavish way. When he said 'This is the beautiful Ellouise' I felt like a true queen. And while that may sound silly to some people, in that club I was. It's always good to be appreciated and that goes for whatever you do. Here, in this competitive environment with its emphasis on looks and bodies, I was pretty damn thrilled to be regarded as one of the top girls by Peter Stringfellow. And I loved being popular with the customers. I hadn't felt part of something for a long time and now I was not only working, but I was part of an elite group which gave me loads of self-confidence. Inevitably there'd be rumours that if you were one of Peter's girls you were sleeping with him. For the record, I didn't. As for anyone else, that's their business.

Peter didn't have to chase girls: there were lots of girls

who were all over him, desperate to be close to him. One of these was Charlene. There was another girl who didn't particularly like me: an ex-police officer called Kerry who was an astonishing pole dancer with muscles like Madonna's. Kerry was in Charlene's gang and was very open about the fact that she couldn't stand me. I'd never spoken to her. In this line of work it doesn't take a lot to make enemies: money, popularity and youth all inspire jealousy; there will always be something. Any camaraderie between the girls was largely superficial. But it didn't worry me. I quickly realised how things worked. No longer was I the meek little girl who showed up in the appalling floral dress and black shoes – I was now a professional dancer. And the fact that I had enemies proved I was good at what I did. I could compete with anyone out there.

Peter liked to make a big show of things and to publicly acknowledge those who were doing well. Each month there was an Angel of the Month award where one night would be dedicated to the chosen girl: she'd have her own flyers made up, a video of her dancing playing every thirty minutes and an award ceremony at midnight. Peter would get up on stage and officially award the lucky girl the title.

'Tonight I'm greatly honoured to award Ellouise Angel of the Month. She's been with us for about eight months now and – wouldn't you agree? – she's really had an impact. So I want to award Ellouise with this gift from heaven [the cash prize]. Now she is going to honour us with a dance to commemorate her night.' Then the girl, in this case me, would take to the stage and do a solo dance in front of everybody. I don't actually remember much about the dance itself, after getting a kiss and hug from Peter, but I do recall the punters smiling at me and congratulating me – and getting a lot more business.

The money you received for being Angel of the Month was known as 'Heavenly Money' so 20 per cent of it would go back to heaven – otherwise known as the club. (Yes, I know. Go figure.) I have to say that Peter really did treat us like 'angels' though. At Christmas he put on an award ceremony for us, our very own Oscars except that it was called the Angel Awards. He created this world where it was possible to feel like you were truly the most amazing woman on earth, and two months after winning Angel of the Month, I was being awarded Best New Angel of the Year. My award was a gold necklace in the shape of an A (for Angel), with a diamond. I look back and cringe at the cheesiness of it now, but at the time I felt on top of the world. It was the recognition all the girls wanted so when you got it and they didn't, of course that meant you must be sleeping with Peter. I was pretty chuffed actually. I don't care if it wasn't the Oscars because for me it was a huge deal. I'd come into this business not even knowing what I was doing, just a girl with no qualifications looking for a job – which I'd proved to be very good at.

After the 'Angel' ceremony, the awards actually meant that I was required to do additional work for the club in the form of promotions and photoshoots. I would now appear on all the club flyers and marketing material as well as in Stringfellows' own magazine. Doing this meant fitting in photoshoots with my stripping work since the promotional work was unpaid: the honour of being an Angel was supposed to be payment enough.

Most of the shoots were done in the club itself, or in Peter's flat next door where his huge satin-sheet-covered bed was often the backdrop. I also flew to Mexico with one other Angel and a group of models. We stayed in a private villa with its own beach and our own chef. We had plenty of free time but the reality of being on a shoot like this is that you're restricted in certain ways. You can't shoot in the midday sun so it would usually take place in the early morning. That meant we had to be in makeup for 5am. Meanwhile you couldn't sunbathe as this would give you tan lines or, worse, sunburn, which is a huge no-no for photographs. I found myself stuck in a remote villa, avoiding the sun all day, which isn't really what you want to do when you're in a place like this.

When Peter launched the club's first underwear range, I did photoshoots and flew up North to do an underwear show to promote the line. That's what you'd expect an Angel to do. What you might *not* expect her to do is attend a speech given by the Conservative Party MP Ann Widdecombe. Peter was and is a huge supporter of the Tories and he often lent his backing to their cause. In this case it meant taking along an entourage of girls, of which I was one, in sexy, skimpy cocktail dresses to a very swish dinner at a top London hotel. With everyone else around us sat in appropriately smart business attire, I was so embarrassed that I just stared straight ahead. I didn't even dare look around in case I caught someone's eye. I was too scared to even go to the toilet on my own. All I could think about was what these intelligent, successful, respectable people must be thinking of us, knowing we were strippers. In the end, apart from my huge inferiority complex, I had a good but incredibly surreal evening. It was easily one of the strangest, most bizarre days in my life.

I'd also begun to do some photographic modelling. Dancing had given me so much confidence so I felt that

I could do anything I wanted. I always knew I had something but I'd never felt so good about myself. When men tell you every evening that you're lovely you start to believe it. I found an agency who took me on straight away, a fact which only added to my euphoria. I had some pictures from photoshoots I'd done at Strings but the agency sent me straight out to get some better ones done. It was so exciting; I had to pick out what I had to wear and turn up nice and early – 9am is very early for a stripper – for the makeup artist.

After my preliminary shoot, I started going to castings and was lucky enough to get work immediately. I did a variety of jobs including shoots for lads' mags like *Loaded*, and a variety of calendars and underwear catalogues. They all paid pretty badly compared to what I was used to earning but some of them meant flying to exotic locations like LA, and Portugal. Even the photoshoots in Birmingham and around the UK were exciting to begin with. One of my best shoots was as a body double for Gwyneth Paltrow in the film *Possession*: they needed someone to do a bum-shot scene for one of the main actresses – I wasn't told who – and I got the casting. I was picked up from home in a chauffer-driven Mercedes and taken to the studios where I was given my own (small) trailer. After being told someone would come and get me I was left to relax. There was a TV, books and a fridge full of fruit, snacks and drinks so I was more than happy. Lunchtime came round and I was brought a big tray of food. The day wore on and still no call for work. By about 3.30pm someone came to my trailer and apologised, but 'filming was running late and could you go home and we'll see you tomorrow'.

Tomorrow came and so did the car. I was picked up at 7am and taken to my trailer, where I sat until 2 or 3pm until someone sent me home. After that they said I didn't need to come in the next day: from here on I'd be on standby, which meant I was to be available at short notice to be at the studio. I was on standby for another two days when I got a call saying they'd cut the scene and I wouldn't be needed after all. No problem: I was getting paid £800 a day for each day, regardless of what happened or didn't. Plus I got to see a major movie studio, be driven around by a chauffer, feel like a star in a trailer and be part of the general buzz.

It was one of the easiest jobs I had ever done. Other good jobs were the front cover for a music magazine called *Kingsize* with Kid Rock: we did the shoot in a posh London hotel. Makeup took hours – I was given the heaviest eye makeup and the biggest hair. When Kid Rock turned up the shoot was done at record speed; there were no changes for him. He just walked in and stood there so we had to be directed around him. We did just three shots and he was gone. He didn't say a word to anyone apart from his entourage and had the worst body odour ever – which was unfortunate for me as one of my shots meant I had to have my head within centimetres of his armpit!

Another great shoot was an ad for Burtons with Martin Kemp at Pinewood Studios. It started off as the most boring day: me and another model sitting in a trailer dressed in Santa outfits (mid-summer) where we waited for eight mind-numbing hours. Eventually we got to do our shoot with Martin Kemp, who was lovely; a genuinely nice guy with no airs and graces. He chatted with the runners, the tea lady and us – treating everyone as equals – and he really made my day. Up till this point the only 'celebrities' I'd met had been seriously unimpressive in terms of their (lack of) people skills but he was so refreshing. Unfortunately we ended up as barely recognisable blurs in the background of the shoot, which was a shame because it appeared on a billboard, but I still enjoyed the experience. Other shoots were for music magazines, music videos, extras work and bit-parts for slightly naff TV shows that nobody talks about now.

Modelling was fun and a huge ego boost but I soon realised that on very rare occasions one model would break through and have a lucrative career. Some were well paid (like the body-double work I did) but more often than not the jobs we were all chasing were for £150–£250, which is not a lot for being part of the demeaning casting process. At first the castings were all part of the job and I found it exciting, going to different studios or meeting magazine editors. Then it just became hard work. It's no fun traipsing all over London after only four hours' sleep, knowing you might only have an outside chance of getting the job, seeing as you'd be up against 30 or 40 other girls. Plus I was still working full time at Strings.

I was getting bored with the long arduous waits and hanging around with the most dull, draining girls who spent all their time boasting about who'd done which shoot and who was dating which footballer (the models were ten times worse than strippers). Some of the photographers were just mean and would be constantly criticising you: 'I thought you were much thinner, your pictures must be deceptive'. Or they'd be screaming – literally – for the makeup artist to do something about a girl's awful skin or terrible hair when the poor girl was no more than a foot away. Then they'd just bark orders at you in dictator-like fashion until every inch of your body was in the most uncomfortable but apparently perfect stance. For me modelling wasn't that glamorous at all: for all the castings, long days and demanding photoshoots, the rewards weren't that great. Sure it might give you a fast route to dubious celebrity status but I wasn't interested in that. Money and financial security were my goals and that's where stripping won hands down.

Chapter 6

Russian eggs and a Chinese proposal

My pictures were everywhere, I had a few well-paying regulars and I was earning very good money while sipping champagne. After two years at Strings a bad night would mean earning maybe £300, an average night could be anything from £400 to £800 and an amazing night meant anything over £1,000. Of course you could always go home in debt to the club if things were slow. There were also lots of gifts and extras. One regular, a little Chinese guy, would come once or twice a week, buy me dinner, usually lobster salad – my dish of choice – and champagne. He bought me gifts and paid me well for my time. I was really fortunate as he never pushed to see me out of work hours like many of the regulars did.

He was the start of a string of regulars, some good, others not so desirable.

There was one called Peter, a young guy with a wife and kids who used to come in at least once a fortnight, sometimes weekly, and spend six to eight hundred pounds a time. After about five or six months, he broke down crying, 'I'm in debt, big debt. I don't know what to do.'

'What do you mean? What happened?'

'I'm in thousands of pounds of debt from coming in here to see you.'

I sat aghast, not knowing what to say.

'But you're a banker, you earn so much, how did you get into debt?'

'I'm not a banker … my wife doesn't know about any of this. What should I do?'

That was a question I couldn't answer.

He was basically telling me he was addicted to the club and had thousands of pounds of debt because of seeing *me*. He'd told me he was a wealthy banker but it was all a lie.

His confessions were distressing and made me feel like shit. He'd always made out he was really well paid and never gave any hint that he couldn't afford coming to the club. I felt awful for ages but eventually I came to realise it was his responsibility: he knew he had a problem and yet he kept coming in. I would send him home and refuse to sit with him or dance for him hoping it would sour the experience of the club for him. It didn't. After a few weeks of me spurning him he gave up on me and just started to obsess over someone else and waste more money. I lost all sympathy for him. But there was no way I could carry on taking money from him knowing I was adding to his troubles.

There was one girl whose client proposed to her by bringing her Matryushka – Russian nesting dolls – which she opened one by one. The last one contained a large diamond. I'm not sure if she agreed to marry him but I'm pretty sure she kept the stone. I had a proposal once, but it was far less romantic. He was a Chinese customer (I seemed to attract Chinese men; they love blondes), a lovely guy in his early forties who was reasonably rich. He'd come in early in the night once or twice a week, which was very thoughtful, since early evening was a quiet time and this way I could earn money. After a few months he asked me if I wanted to stop dancing. I'd give him my stock answer – of course, doesn't everyone? – until one day he asked me to marry him.

'You don't really like this job, do you, Ellouise ... I mean it's not really what you want to do, is it?'

'Of course it's not my first career choice but my

choices are pretty limited right now.' (Not to mention that I earn shitloads of money.)

'You can do so much more than this; I want to give to you more than this. Marry me ... (long pause) ... You could live with me, never have to worry about rent and bills again, never have to worry about money again. I can take care of you. You could do what you want with your life, never dance again ...'

It was unbearable. He was half-sitting, half-kneeling in this unexpected and very unwanted proposal.

'I can't marry you. I don't love you. I love spending time with you and we're great friends but I can't marry you.'

I signalled for him to get up from his semi-kneeling pose. God, it was so embarrassing. I continued, 'You shouldn't be wasting your time in strip clubs. You have so much to offer, you're a great catch. You need to be out there in the real world looking for someone. You'll never find your soul mate in here.'

He looked devastated. I told him not to come in any more; he had too much to offer and shouldn't waste any more time in strip clubs. I knew in doing this I was losing a very good customer but I'm not in the business of ruining someone's life. After this he came less frequently and we'd have a drink and a catch up but I refused to take money from him.

Some gifts were weird – like the guy who turned up and gave me Norton Anti-Virus software. I didn't know him. He just walked in, gave me the software and then walked out again. He'd made the assumption that I owned a computer, which I didn't. Even as late as seven years ago, computers weren't all that common. The only people I knew who had them worked in offices. It was a very strange gift to give a stripper, especially when you a) didn't know her and b) had no idea whether she owned a computer or not. I just thanked him and he disappeared.

There was a guy we called the Fabergé Egg Guy, who came to see Miranda, a much older girl who'd been dancing a long time and was good at her job. He was a very wealthy Russian and he loved her. Every time he came to London he'd bring her a Fabergé-style jewelled egg – if you've never seen them, they're ornamental eggs encrusted with semi-precious and precious stones. I'm not sure whether the eggs were real Fabergé eggs, but they were valuable none the less. Miranda figured this after the first one so told him she'd decided to collect them. Naturally she sold them. She even claimed to have sold one for several thousand pounds.

While we all loved getting presents (although I'm not so sure about the Norton Anti-Virus software), there was nothing a girl liked more than money, and many of the girls needed lots of it just to keep up appearances. My upkeep was pretty low-key compared to many of the other strippers, who spent the GDP of a small African country grooming every millimetre of their bodies.

Let's start with hair. This ranges from fortnightly colouring at anything from £60–£150 on top of the cost of styling and cuts. Lots of girls have hair extensions that are done every six to eight weeks and can cost in excess of £600 – some are cheaper, but you can tell! There are also hair pieces that are usually cheaper than extensions but can still cost close to £100, as well as expensive human hair wigs. It was nothing for some girls to visit the hairdresser three times a week just to have their hair blow dried. This cost at least £40 a time. As is often the case, it's the high-maintenance girls who often have the worst hair as they've processed the life out of it. While they got their hair done, they often had their nails done at the same time. This might be anything from French manicures at £35 a pop to false nails and toenails. Yes, I did say false toenails.

Tanning is very important, not only to look bronzed and glowing but also because a tan hides a multitude of sins: cellulite, stretch marks, scars, bruising, not to mention that when you have a tan you instantly appear to have dropped a dress size. Of course there were girls who overdid it and ended up almost permanently orange. Some girls would regularly use sunbeds but for the ultimate orange glow, a lot of girls would have fake tan applied on a weekly basis at £40 a pop. Excessive? Possibly, but then there was a lot about this business that was over the top. I know of quite a few girls who have sunbeds in their homes but this doesn't stop them indulging in several beach holidays each year.

And then there's makeup. I know girls with cupboards bursting with jars and tubes of Chanel, Dior, YSL, MAC – much of it barely used or unopened. I'm not big on spending loads on eye shadow and lip gloss and think the big brands are just a rip off. Rimmel and Maybelline are fine and do the job just as well. There are some girls who are addicted to it and have no idea when enough is enough. They can go through stuff in a matter of weeks that would last me six months. And they're absolute suckers for the latest revolutionary face cream. I'm afraid I'm just as easily led in that regard and, like many of the other girls, I'm a Crème De La Mer junkie. Perfume is another big expense, along with body creams, as a girl can go through at least a bottle of perfume a fortnight. And then there's the all-important glitter which most strippers lavish all over their body – and which many men have worn home only to be caught out.

Of course, a stripper needs to do something about her body hair. Where to start? Leg waxing, arm waxing, underarms, toes, eyebrows, top lip – all these body parts have to be attended to. When I started at Strings you didn't take your G-string off, but now, as in most clubs, the girls do. A girl would start with waxing her bikini line. She might decide to dye the remaining pubic hair or have it shaped, or both. One girl had a pink heart. The beautician bleached her natural hair then dyed it pink (warning: don't use normal dye or you could injure yourself!). This cost around £60 but being such a precise shape it needs maintenance on a weekly basis. Some girls couldn't be bothered waxing all the time so they had their pubic hair lasered, which was even more expensive back then that it is now. A friend of mine did it – then had a butterfly tattoo put there instead, which I thought looked rather good.

Once a girl starts earning decent money it's easy to get seduced by the idea of spas and luxury treatments. This could be anything from weekly massages, facials, reflexology, hot stone therapy, mud baths and flotation tanks to things like microdermabrasion (just £700 for a course of ten), chemical peels (even more money), oxygen facials and blue algae treatments. She might go on a £700 weekend to Champneys Spa or blow £5,000 on something more serene in Indonesia.

Teeth whitening is popular and many of the girls had it done more than once a year. Then there were slimming treatments and of course Botox and collagen injections to plump up lips. Most of the girls will deny they've had anything done but you know they're spending between £400 and £600 every three to four months.

You might ask whether it was all worth it. Among strippers body image is everything: it was important to look good and feel good when you were dancing, but at the same time a lot of girls had a distorted view of their bodies, which I suppose is not surprising. It's easy for some, especially the older ones, to get paranoid when new girls arrive. Many of them went too far, in my view, and simply lost the plot. Nowhere was this more evident than in the use of cosmetic surgery. If it could be shaped, enhanced, made bigger, smaller, removed or sucked out it was. Many girls have had more than one boob job, not because they need to do the ten-year switch (after ten years, implants need to be replaced) but because after a year or two they just want them bigger. Certain cultures seemed to be more obsessed by surgery than others: Brazil, for example. It was fairly routine for a Brazilian girl to 'go home' for a few months and return two dress sizes smaller, with enormous breasts and a very pert, tight bottom.

Some girls were open about their surgery. Take Nicola. She's a slightly older girl and has probably had more work done than anyone else I know. She started off as an air hostess for Virgin but the lure of stripping was too strong and sucked her in. She got into it later in life and has to be one of the biggest personalities I've ever met. She's had everything done: a full-on boob job, some sort of eyelid surgery, £10,000 worth of teeth, and fillers and Botox pumped into her to give her that all-important youthful appearance. You can tell she's had work but I think she looks great and it suits her big, bold personality. She's also genuine – she'll openly tell you which are her bits and which are the surgeon's, although I'm surprised she can remember.

Beauty expenditure isn't the only reason that many strippers have nothing to show for their years of work, even when they've been earning big money. Not surprisingly drugs were popular with a lot of girls. Cocaine was the number-one choice with diazepam also used frequently. These were used during the shift. When the girls went out there'd be all sorts of other drugs – Ecstasy, more coke, you name it – and it'd add up to a very expensive night out. Alcohol was also popular. Some of the girls didn't wait for customers to buy it for them: they spent a load at the bar themselves. Quite often they were so wasted they couldn't hustle and ended up making a loss for that evening. I've known girls drink two bottles of wine daily at work. The champagne whores were the worst. These were girls who wanted to live the lives of their customers after work. They'd go to pretentious nightclubs in central London – Chinawhites was popular – and buy bottle after bottle at £120 a throw.

I've known a fair few girls who didn't even have enough money at the end of the month to pay their rent. To make matters worse they rented luxury apartments in places like Hampstead and Kensington. They had no sense of value and were just draining themselves. You'd hear them moaning about having to pay £1,500 a month in rent, but it was their choice. Meanwhile I was paying £500 a month in North London. It wasn't glamorous, it wasn't cool but it was all I needed. I didn't spend a lot, either. Unlike other strippers I wasn't a fan of designer bags with huge diamante logos or buckles. These are a bit of a signature for strippers – they love a big logo – as are Jimmy Choo shoes and designer watches. As far as I was concerned it was all an absolute waste of hard-earned cash. I had the same attitude to my work outfits. Many girls obsessed over these but I took the view that the guys didn't care how much you spent as long as your outfit looked sexy and worked on you. For me, spending £200 in Agent Provocateur on one costume was ridiculous. I knew I looked just as good and could earn the same in a £30 set from Ann Summers or something from La Senza.

Over the course of a year, if you throw in the personal trainer, two holidays, extensions done seven times a year, highlights done 12 times a year, a piece or two of plastic surgery, four trips for Botox, two designer hand-bags, several pairs of Jimmy Choos, a few shopping sprees in Selfridges, teeth bleaching, a spa trip, seven or eight facials, monthly massages, bimonthly trips to the nail salon, weekly trips for tanning and expensive costumes, you still wouldn't have accounted for the makeup and skin products, drugs, alcohol, travel, rent and bills. So it meant that the really high-maintenance girls needed to earn 60 grand a year just to break even – no wonder some girls can earn good money for ten years and have nothing to show for it.

I went through a fad of having highlights until I realised my natural hair colour was far better and made me look less like a stripper. I have always cut my own hair and stuck to that – probably not the wisest thing to do, but the few times a hairdresser cut my hair I was seriously unimpressed. I've always spent money on tanning as it is an integral part of the job although a subtle, natural tan was my choice and limited the money I spent. Other than that my grooming regime was nonexistent and my outgoings limited. It wasn't because I was too tight or thought I didn't need to; I just knew that the non-stripper thing worked for me and I really didn't want to be thought of as a stripper outside of work. To this day I use my little tricks and stripper secrets but never spend money on my appearance.

Up until now all my money had gone on starting my life as a stripper – the clothes, shoes, makeup and perfume as well as setting up a home. Now, seeing the reality of the stripping world and the girls in it, I decided I didn't want to be stuck here for ever like some of them seemed to be. This was a chance to earn really good money, set myself up financially and use it to get out of stripping.

Chapter 7

◦◦

So you want to be a stripper?

There are a lot of girls out there – and maybe you're one of them – who think that stripping is easy money and that they can do it without it affecting them in some way. I suppose that some of this has been perpetuated by stories in various tabloids about so-called 'nice girls' from a 'good background' who strip for a couple of years, make loads of money and then finish their post-graduate studies, get a high-flying job and settle down to a respectable middle-class life. In all my years stripping I didn't come across many students who were dancing to pay for their doctorates. While there might be girls who start stripping when they're students, most of them don't remain so after becoming strippers. For one reason or another, the lifestyle sucks them in and they give up their studies. It would take a hell of a lot of discipline to be a student, even part-time, and make a good living as a stripper.

So you want to be a stripper?

What does it take to be good at stripping? When I talk about being 'good' at it I mean being able to work, earn money and not get sucked in by the fantasy that is a big part of it. This is a business and you have to have your business brain on when you're doing it. A good stripper is one who can earn a lot of money while maintaining her sanity, her self-respect, her health and her sense of perspective.

Over the years I've seen a lot of girls come in to stripping but they don't do very well, simply because they don't have the right mentality. For starters, you need to forget about who you are when you're working and play a role. What role? Well, any role that you think is required to get the most money out of the guy. And that means you need to be very instinctive and a good judge of character. Some girls can do it really well while others, even after several years, still don't know how. It's not dissimilar to a salesperson in a boutique being able to figure out who they can manipulate into buying more than one item. The skill set is exactly the same, except that in my case I'm observing my customer from the stage or on the floor at a short distance. Even before I speak to him I'm figuring out who he is and what makes him tick.

A lot of girls think it sounds easy but often they don't have the attitude for the environment. First of all, you have to be a damn good actress, and you have to be able to turn it on in a heartbeat. Your ability to tune in to your audience and your customers is directly related to making money. Forget being acrobatic on the pole: that might impress some but I wasn't that good on it and it never held me back. What I had was instinct and good judgement. Sure, a good body helped as well; I was grateful for that. My friends often said they'd never seen someone who could read a client so well. And because of that I wasted less time with low-paying clients and spent more time with the ones that forked out. I knew that my innocent, fresh appearance was my personal selling point so I played to my strengths and stuck to it. Many girls are confused or simply haven't thought it through enough so they're not really projecting a clear image that guys can easily latch on to.

You also need to be thick-skinned because you'll have to take criticism, abuse and general nastiness from both customers and the girls you work with. There are lots of guys who are so embarrassed at being turned down for a fuck that they'll just start abusing you, even though they shouldn't have asked in the first place. After a while it just rolls off you – at least it did with me. I just took it as part of the deal … most of the time. A lot of the girls were nasty because they were jealous or insecure. I'm not naturally a jealous person, partly because

I tend to focus on what I'm doing, but it's extremely difficult for a lot of girls to not envy others. Frankly, if you are the jealous type, you shouldn't even consider it. It will ruin you.

I've always had a strong sense of reality and therefore had no trouble separating the club from the rest of my life and I think that helped me keep things in perspective. Yes, the work was real but the person I was inside the club was only part of me: it was an act that I put on in much the same way as a lawyer or banker adopts a different façade for their job from the person they are at home. Unfortunately a lot of girls get so carried away with life in the club they carry it on outside and completely lose touch with who they are. In many cases they're not that mentally stable in the first place and stripping – and the lifestyle, drugs and partying that come with it – can tip them over the edge.

Finally I think you need to have a hunger for money: it must unquestionably be your first priority. You might find this surprising – don't all strippers do it for money? Well, yes and no. They might start off with that mindset but sometimes they get seduced by the adulation – or what they see as adulation – and then they forget why they're there. Some of them will actually work for a loss just to be on that stage! I kid you not.

The more I got to know the business, the more I saw

its negative side. At the end of the night the girls would rush into the changing room, desperate to go home to sleep, go out and party or meet the customer who's waiting around the corner in a taxi. But there were always the same few girls left on the floor in the most godawful state. They were so trashed they didn't even realise the night was over. You knew they'd drunk enormous amounts, taken shedloads of coke and MDMA and were totally wasted. They just lay there with their shoes off, makeup smudged, and looked so desperate.

One night it was someone's birthday and a group of girls were going to a club. I wasn't that keen but, wanting to fit in, I went along. One of the girls, an infamous drunk, was already so trashed she could hardly walk but the club let her in as she was a regular and these girls spent a fair bit of money on champagne. So there she was on the crowded dance floor in her mini dress and suddenly she took off her knickers, removed her tampon, threw it across the room and did the splits on the dance floor. Someone helped her to her feet only for her to walk over to the table, throw her knickers into the ice bucket and throw up all over herself. I couldn't take it. This just wasn't me so I got my stuff and left. I later found out she'd been asked to leave and was unable to walk so the door staff carried her out. She'd then lain unconscious on the footpath – still knickerless – so the club called the police. It gets worse. Apparently she was trying to feel up the policeman who must've felt sorry for her because he took her to the station until she sobered up and let her go without charge – so she said. She'd been done for drink driving a few weeks earlier.

Another year flew past; I was earning really well at this point, and life was good. My modelling was taking off, I had nice clothes and a group of acquaintances from the club to go out with. Then Peter Stringfellow decided to put together a girl band and asked me to be in it. One of his friends was a music agent, and they came up with the idea to put together a Strings girl band. If you've ever wondered how crappy bands get formed, now you know!

I was taken to the studio to sing a verse or two to make sure I wasn't tone deaf, although I was probably not far off. I was the second girl chosen and one of my friends in the club, Isis, was next. The third girl wasn't a stripper: she worked as a go-go dancer on weekends and looked down her nose at strippers so, not surprisingly, we didn't get on with her. We still needed a fourth. Peter tried a few girls but he just couldn't settle on one. I asked him to listen to my friend Tamara simply by having her come to his table at Strings one night. He was immediately sold on her – she has the most amazing singing voice – and she didn't even have to go to the studio for a test.

Tamara became our lead singer – well, one of us had to have a voice. Before we knew it we were meeting stylists who dressed us in cheesy white and gold ensembles. Then it was off to a photoshoot followed by the recording of the most terrible song that made us all cringe. At the same time we were caught up in all the hype. The next thing we knew, we had a deal for one single with Universal Records and then it was off to Corfu to shoot the video – it was all happening at record speed. We stayed in the best hotel, had a massive team to look after us and had great fun. The video itself was gruelling work; we had the worst choreographer and were really unhappy with the silly moves we had to do.

We had to shoot our dance parts one at a time, barefoot on the sand. I was last so by the time it was my turn, the sand was like hot coals: you couldn't walk on it, let alone dance for twenty minutes. But I was overruled; we were on a tight schedule, which left me flustered and my dance was pretty terrible. That night we made up for it and went clubbing. Apparently the biggest club of the area had heard that a pop group was shooting a video and invited us down. We all felt like superstars and it was really surreal so we did what anyone else would do and sat in the VIP area sipping champagne until our manager sent us home slightly tipsy as we had another early start the next day. We were there about three days, during which time Peter came over for one night and took us all out for dinner.

Then it was back to the real world. When we returned things had slowed down. We were still doing interviews and photoshoots but the buzz had gone. The fourth girl – who we decided really had a broomstick up her arse – was constantly all over the manager and probably telling him every word we said. We suspected she was having a fling with him and before long she was being given prominence in the photoshoots and the sexiest outfits. She didn't talk to us or socialise with us. It was a nightmare. It ended the way a lot of manufactured bands end: the single was never released and we were dropped by the label. In retrospect I'm glad as we would have been the laughing-stock of the music industry. I didn't see this at the time as I was too caught up in my nonexistent stardom, but today I thank my lucky stars.

When we broke up I wasn't at all bothered. I had no aspirations to ever be a singer and, unlike Tamara, I couldn't sing a note. It ended up being a great experience, mainly because I did it with my closest friends, but when we returned from the video shoot back to the real world, it all looked less appealing. Now I was back to working five nights a week, doing stuff for the band two or three days a week as well as my own modelling and modelling for the club. I realised I wasn't having fun any more. I wasn't sleeping and I felt like I was drowning in it all. I had no time for me and my health began to suffer. I was averaging four hours' sleep a night so after two or three months of this, I was exhausted, irritable and constantly on edge.

It just felt that I was giving away far too much of myself and I had nothing left for me. There were a few times when I asked to go home early, but the manager would make a huge fuss and refuse. One night I'd been working for the club all day and was absolutely dead on my feet. I had to work again the next morning on some promotional stuff but I just couldn't do it. The manager was being an utter arsehole and wouldn't listen to me. I knew I physically and mentally couldn't keep up with the workload any more. Something just snapped that day. I went to the changing room and packed my bag. I picked it up and walked past him without saying a word. I'm sure when he saw me walking out he must've thought I was having a tantrum and bluffing. But I wasn't. I was burned out.

I was sad to leave Strings and for a while I was very emotional about it, even though I knew I'd made the right decision. I'd made some great friends there and after three years it'd become a second home to me. I'd gone in as a young girl and emerged as a young woman, who, though naïve in some ways, was far smarter about herself and the world. Mostly, I'd made a life for myself, and created opportunities. I was the only person in control of me and leaving Strings was another way of showing it.

I did nothing for a few weeks: I was simply too tired. Then I realised I had time, money and freedom. I took exotic holidays, dedicated myself to my modelling and started doing some acting. I went through a short spate of clubbing but I hated it. The whole central London night-club scene is full of wannabes and Z-list celebrities. With them come the hoards of gold-digging, wannabe famous women. Maybe I was just getting a little older and wiser, but I realised what a load of crap it was one day and never went again. I've never had any interest in dating someone famous, particularly a footballer – God forbid! From what I've seen, it's more hassle than it's worth.

Chapter 8

❧

'Do I get sex with that dance?'

I'm well aware there are people who think prostitution and stripping are intertwined. I imagine the thinking goes something like: 'Strippers take their clothes off in front of men for money, which exploits them in the same way as prostitution.' Let me tell you it's a pretty big step from dancing in front of men naked, to having sex with them for money. And yes, it's a lot easier for a girl in a strip club to meet the kind of men who will offer her money for sex after-hours. But that doesn't automatically make strippers prostitutes – actually, a lot of them are quite the opposite, almost prudish. There are guys on dating sites looking for the same thing and girls who will supply it.

The fact is there are always men who will pay for sex

and there are women who are happy to be paid. And some of those happen to be strippers. As a business of course, the industry is pretty careful not to allow prostitution to happen on the premises. It's likely that a stripper will meet a man at the club, get to know him and their business will continue away from the club. It's nothing to do with the club, which will usually have strict policies about prostitution – certainly Strings did. But when they walk through the door and leave, the girls are free to meet who they want – unless the club gets wind of it and then they may find themselves sacked.

Generally I'd say there are two types of strippers who engage in prostitution: the 'Working Girls' and the 'In Denials'. Note that 'In Denials' can cross over to become 'Working Girls'.

Working Girls

She's working and she's earning money. In her mind it's as simple as that. She sees it as no more than a business transaction: she agrees a sum, does the job and gets paid for it. She's fully aware of what she's doing and has accepted it; however, she'll never admit it to anyone.

The girls who become working girls are often big earners already. They tend to be foreign – and will stop at nothing to make as much money as they can. Is it a cultural thing? I don't know. But don't get me wrong – there are plenty of English girls doing it too. It's just that some of the foreign girls are incredibly single-minded about it and quite ruthless. You'll see them in the VIP area, where they will be among the big moneymen. They'll have regulars who are wealthy and who come in night after night and spend a packet – knowing they will get something when they leave the club. These girls are looking for the fastest way to shore up their bank accounts. Frankly if you offered them a chance to do it another way, they'd probably be into that too. To them it's just business, and lucrative business at that.

I've known a couple of girls like that who gave me my very first experience of being close to prostitution. (One went on to marry a very famous DJ.) It happened when I was at Strings. I was sat with a punter and two English girls with their customers. One of the girls leant over to me and said, 'It's cool, we've organised one and a half grand for the night.'

I was stunned. 'Wow. One and a half grand to sit with these guys is pretty amazing.'

The girl looked at me like I was an idiot and said, 'No, for the whole night. After we leave here.' When it eventually dawned on me I was so shocked, I made a swift exit. A lot of girls will use sit-downs to work out their deals with the customer for the rest of the night. If a girl is sat with a customer for extended periods of time or the same guy over and over, it generally tends to be because he may be getting extracurricular activity – or at the very least, he's hoping!

Of course men will ask. You get it all the time and it's naïve for anyone to say it doesn't happen. A notoriously rich customer once asked me and another girl to sit with him; he was constantly asking us to go back to his hotel and was offering obscene amounts of money. We both refused on several occasions. Then I was called to the stage. On my return, he no longer wanted my company, just the other, young Brazilian girl. When my shift finished, I got in the taxi with my usual driver and left. He pulled over on a nearby street, a minute from the club, as his radio was going crazy, and who did I see walking with arms around each other but the customer and the young Brazilian girl. She had obviously had a change of heart when I was on stage. No wonder he didn't want me any more!

A friend of mine would only have sex with one customer, a long-term regular who gave her a monthly allowance. I have no idea what the amount was but it must have been pretty high for her even to consider it. She would never dream of shagging some random punter after work, whatever the fee. But she'd known this guy for a while, he was in no way disgusting – he was rather attractive actually – and it was clearly an offer she felt she couldn't refuse. Occasionally, a guy will give a girl an allowance in return for a sexual relationship, rather than a one-off shag. This usually happens with girls who don't put it about and would never consider prostitution. It's more like being a paid mistress. In fact that's exactly what it is, although I bet paid mistresses wouldn't want to hear that they're on a par with a stripper. The double standards that exist, even between women, never cease to amaze me.

Another time when I was at Strings, this creepy little guy who always wore the same clothes and looked like he rarely washed became a sort of regular. I say sort of as he only visited for a few weeks before making me an offer I could easily refuse! He said he would pay me a grand a month if we could have 'an arrangement'. I knew exactly what he meant but just wanted him to say it. He wanted to pop round to my place on occa-sion, once a week or so in return for a grand a month. I sat there very quiet for a while, and he mentioned that was a sum of twelve grand a year – just in case I couldn't add up. I politely declined. He asked me to think about it and if I ever changed my mind etc. etc. ... as if he was not just offering me what he clearly saw was an astronomical sum but that this was also the opportunity of a lifetime and I'd be mad to turn it down.

I knew one girl who would make a very large amount of money on sit-downs and would have the same guys coming time and time again. She was much older and not overly attractive. I never really understood how she earned quite so much until one day I was told she was a hooker. From that day I started to watch her a bit more carefully and had to kick myself for not being able to work that one out for myself. She never kept it a secret – among the girls anyway – and if asked would talk about it openly, although I personally never dared ask her. It was her business and she made a lot of money. She wasn't ashamed of it so felt no need to hide it from anyone – apart from the club, that is.

There's always a lot of gossip about one girl or another being a hooker but in this world it's nearly impossible to separate the truth from slanderous talk. There are girls who hide it so well that when they get sacked for prostitution you're in shock because you thought you were friends and therefore knew her. This happened with one girl I was friends with and really liked. She was a young, intelligent Brazilian girl who was studying and was really together. Claiming she was 'sick' she went home mid-shift one night and shortly after was followed out by her customer. The manager was a tad suspicious and followed the punter to find her waiting in a doorway for him a few streets away. She was promptly sacked the next day, much to my surprise. This in no way affected my opinion of her: she was doing something I was in no way willing to do but it's her decision and her body.

Sometimes you learn about prostitution from the customers, which is always enlightening.

'How much for the night?'

'Sorry, it's not that kind of place here.'

'Yeah right.'

'What's that supposed to mean?'

'Come on, love, name your price, you all have one.'

'I don't, so stop being an arsehole.'

'Oh calm down, sorry love, well most of you have a price, anyway.'

I was getting very irate now. 'What's that supposed to mean?' Then he went on to proudly give me full details of the girls he'd shagged, one or two of them being my friends.

In Denials

These are the girls in complete denial. Usually they don't get a direct payment or a prearranged amount so they won't admit to themselves that it's prostitution. Usually they meet the guy at work and go home with them to 'party' on the promise of a few grams of coke. They end up shagging the guy and the next morning getting their cab fare home (which is always way more than it would ever be).

There are the girls who are taken on shopping sprees and to dinner and expensive West End shows by their regulars and 'fall' into bed with them. Because there is no money changing hands, these girls will never see it as prostitution. Even though the guys are coming in regularly, paying them large sums of money for lap-dances and VIP, taking them shopping and even buying them cars, they still think it's not transactional sex. Any girl who sleeps with a customer and gets something in return, whether it be cash, the customer coming in regularly to spend large amounts of money, shopping sprees, rent payments, cars, two grams of coke or a hundred quid left for their cab fare home (when they live three miles away) is just a hooker in denial in my opinion!

Nadia was a lovely girl with a huge coke habit. She was loud and crazy and slept with everyone and the whole club knew it: she was too wasted to ever be subtle. She would start partying with a group of young guys, drinking and taking drugs. If she was lucky she would get them to the VIP area where she would get even more wasted and nearly every night she'd end up with one guy or another, usually on the premise that she would carrying on partying at his house as he could get more coke (or she was just so out of it she'd shag anyone). It got to the point where she'd shagged her way through everyone who worked there, not just the customers. Needless to say she got sacked.

Amanda had a much sadder story. She was a friend of mine who'd just arrived in England when she started working with me at a club I worked in after leaving Strings. She was just lovely, a beautiful girl with a huge personality and aspirations of becoming a singer. She started drinking and getting way too pissed at work, then she was introduced to coke. She took to it too well and too quickly. She was constantly high and became thin to the point of anorexia. She looked a state. She would have big arguments with girls, customers and management and no one – not for lack of trying – could help her. She too got the sack. I would see her from time to time and she was up and down, sometimes looking great and cleaning up her act, sometimes a mess. About six months later, after I'd changed clubs again, she ended up at the same one I was at.

She soon got herself a bad reputation. One day she was caught out by the bosses. She'd been sat in the VIP area with a guy, and then asked to go home early because she was 'feeling sick'. Her punter had just left and was overheard telling his friends he'd hooked up. The boss let her go home, sent someone to follow her and she was seen getting into a cab with the guy she had been with in the VIP area. Once again she was sacked. The last I heard and saw she was a prostitute working for a 'dance' place, but I saw the website and believe me there were no dance moves I'd ever seen before in the pictures.

For me there is no amount of money that would make me have sex with a guy. And believe me, I've been offered some serious money. One time a young Arab 'prince' came in with an entourage of about twelve. He picked me and another blonde to join him and we just did dance after dance for him. He hardly spoke to us, just had us drink champagne and dance for each other, while pretending not to watch. Near the end of the night, he asked us to go to his hotel with him. We both said we couldn't so he called over this guy with a briefcase, opened it, took out wads of cash and put two piles on the table. 'Seven thousand pounds each,' he said, 'will be yours if you come back to my hotel.' Now seven grand for a night may sound tempting, but not tempting enough to do what he wanted. We both gracefully declined so he paid us for the night and left. We'd still been given more than a thousand pounds each for that night so I was more than happy!

As for stripping being exploitative, well yes it is – but in most cases it only exploits the men who part with their cash to see it. A girl who has her wits about her and can navigate her way through the bright lights, the long hours, the male adulation and ultimately hang on to the money can do very well indeed. While stripping was full of temptation, the fact that some girls do fall victim to the lure of drugs and prostitution should not, I think, be seen as a direct result of their involvement in stripping, but rather of their own individual characters.

Chapter 9

‿✑

Not so happy families

I'll tell you something that surprised me at first but it shouldn't have really. A lot of strippers have had less than ideal home lives. By that I mean they often come from broken homes, although that could be said for a lot of the population! My early childhood was good. Although at the time I didn't think it, my mum was doing the best for me. She was pushy and strict and so I had a highly disciplined upbringing. As well as being strongly academic, I was an accomplished dancer and musician, and won awards for my Irish dancing from the age of five. Little did I know then how I'd be using my dancing skills.

I represented my school and even my county in music and sports, and was always in the top 10 per cent. Thanks to Mum, this went on until I was 14, so I had a pretty happy and uneventful childhood. While my friends were out shopping and meeting boys, I'd be at home studying, being tutored or taking some class or another. At the time I often hated it, but on reflection – and seeing today's teens – I'm happy I had a strict and protective mother. It gave me an appreciation of the benefits of education and also gave me the discipline to cope with working in the stripping industry. But it wasn't all work. We often took trips to the coast in our beaten-up old VW van. My mum would put wooden boards in the back with a mattress on top and all our clothes and food underneath and that would be our home for the next two weeks. These are among my fondest memories.

I'm not sure if my dad was around much or if I've just blanked out a lot of memories: my way of dealing with things is to run away or try to forget they ever happened. My few childhood memories of him were in the pub or down the Irish club. I should also mention that I have two sisters. And that's what gave Dad a few problems.

Both my parents had dark complexions but I was born an eleven-pound, blonde-haired, blue-eyed baby. I was actually born with lush black hair that was an inch long. It went on to grow blonde without falling out first, giving me a reverse roots effect. With both my parents being very dark, this caused raised eyebrows, especially because we lived in a tight-knit Irish community and both my sisters were also dark This led to the age-old joke of me being the milkman's daughter. So much so that when I was about five at school, we had to stand up and say what our parents' jobs were. Of course, I said, 'everyone says my dad's the milkman'. Apparently the teacher didn't know whether to laugh or cry! Because I had blonde grandparents, it was never a great concern growing up.

I suppose things changed when I was about 12. From a young age I'd heard gossip about my dad's affairs, mainly to do with the landlady of the local pub. He certainly spent enough time there. Around this time, I remember Mum was no longer sleeping upstairs in their bedroom: she took the downstairs sofa and I now know it wasn't out of choice. I think this had been going on for a while but because Mum had hidden it so well, I wasn't aware of it until their arguments became more frequent and aggressive.

I wasn't quite aware how aggressive until one day, when I was about 14, I was sat in my bedroom with my leg plastered from ankle to hip after a knee injury while Irish dancing when I heard them arguing downstairs.

It sounded much worse than usual and Mum was screaming, so my first instinct was to go downstairs to help her. I ended up falling and getting stuck at the bottom of the stairs head-first, which sounds very comical now. All I could do was watch as my dad threw plates, picture frames, lamps and pretty much anything he could get his hands on at my mum. I watched this scene for what felt like an eternity until the argument died down. Dad went back to the pub and Mum did her usual thing of putting on a brave face. She helped me upstairs while pretending nothing had happened and afterwards we never spoke about it. My older sister was married and had left home by now and my middle sister was four years older than me and was always out. Mostly it was just me waking up in the middle of the night to blazing rows whenever my dad decided to grace us with his presence after a night in the pub.

I don't know if the rows got worse or if they were no longer hidden, but the next eight months or so carried on in this manner until everything in the house was either glued or sellotaped together. When you looked around there wasn't anything that wasn't broken – lamps, pictures, the remote control – you name it, it was broken. When Dad was home the arguments were constant so it was almost better that he wasn't. If it all suddenly went off when I was downstairs and I couldn't reach the sanctuary of my bedroom I would sit under the kitchen table until the storm had passed. Under here

I was safe from flying objects – and I could safely reach the bottom cupboard where the biscuits were stored (I was nothing if not resourceful). One day my parents were arguing and my dad chased my mum out of the house while throwing stuff at her. When she got outside he continued to throw bricks, plant pots and stones. She got into her car and drove away. He chased her halfway down the road, gave up and went to the pub.

She never came back.

My life soon changed. From here on I would do anything I could to avoid my father. I would go out drinking every weekend and with no curfews or restrictions, sometimes I wouldn't return home till Monday. I would stay at a friend's house, sleep in the park or stay round a 'boyfriend's' house. I was never questioned or reprimanded, which wasn't surprising since Dad didn't care about me. I was 15, had no self-esteem, felt totally unloved and uncared for. I started hanging round with an older crowd, going to all-night raves, taking up to six Ecstasy tablets in a night and coming home the next day or the day after. The thing is that deep down I didn't want to do it and knew it wasn't good for me. But it's interesting how your life can turn on just one event. You read about kids now and think, 'How did they end up so messed up?' It's not hard to do. Without Mum around, any sense of the life I'd had before evaporated and I just felt there was no point. I couldn't live with Mum since she had no home and was sleeping on the sofa at her work.

I rarely missed school but on the days I did stay home, Dad would shout and abuse me. I use the word abuse now, but honestly, at the time it didn't seem that big a deal because I was in it. In my denial – and maybe this was part of my survival instinct – I told myself (and to this day sometimes still do) that he never abused me as he never actually punched or hit me. He did once throw me fully clothed into a bath of hot water, and held my head under. I realised pretty quickly I was in a hopeless situation. I couldn't leave home as I was too young and had nowhere to go. I didn't tell my mum: although I loved her, I resented her for leaving me and blamed her for a lot of what was happening, so I pushed her away. To this day she still doesn't know the whole story.

Dad stole things from me as well. I had a treasured collection of jewellery, including an antique gold coin my mum had given me, a crystal globe bracelet from my teacher for getting high marks in the eleven plus, items from my grandparents – all of whom had died – and christening and communion gifts. One day when I came home from school it'd all gone. I was upset but I was also smart enough to know I couldn't confront him and so had to let it go. I soon learned that anything of value was no longer safe in my room but, unfortunately, everything had already gone.

To keep my money away from Dad's thieving hands I hung a piece of string down the back of my wardrobe attached at the top by sellotape (it played a big part in my early life) and hung a little pouch at the end of the string so my money was totally hidden. Or so I thought. After about four weeks I found it emptied. Again, what was I supposed to do? I told Mum. Even though she'd never come to the house, she sent round one of her workmates to put a lock on my door while Dad was out, but the door was kicked in the same day.

My sister was rarely around, which didn't help. Even though I was much smaller than her and didn't have much to start with, when she was around she'd borrow my personal items, like clothes, books and shoes. I was constantly getting into trouble at school for turning up without the right things or wearing the wrong clothes. It just made me feel even more isolated.

I began to fear leaving and returning to the house and even leaving my room to go to the bathroom, in case I ran into him. The situation I was in was so unstable – he wasn't rational and even seeing me seemed to anger him. I resorted to drastic measures to avoid him. I'd sit in the bushes across from my house if he or my sister got home before me when I finished school. Sometimes this meant I sat there for over two hours until he went out, usually to the pub. I took to hiding provisions wrapped in plastic in the bushes – a torch, a blanket and a few other bits. I would sit and do my homework or read, anything to pass the time. I also took to peeing in my room, in a bottle that was cut in half, so that I could avoid meeting him in the hallway.

Then one night things got really bad when Dad came home late from the pub. As soon as he entered I heard him. I also heard my sister pleading and sobbing. The next thing I knew, he'd burst into my room, grabbed me by the hair and dragged me downstairs along the floor. He then pulled me off the floor by my hair, grabbed me and started shouting in my face, 'Where is it, where is it?' He was swearing at me now, horrible swearing, and all I could do was cry. I had no idea what was going on. I saw chunks of my hair had come out in his hands and then he held my face so hard I thought my jaw was going to break.

He slapped me and threw me against the radiator, so that I split the top of my head open. Leaving me on the floor, he and my sister went into the kitchen where I heard them put the kettle on. I was dizzy, frightened and sobbing hysterically and still had no idea what I was supposed to have done. Later I found out that Dad had bought my sister a £90 lump of hash. She either used it or sold it but when he came looking for it she must have been so scared she blamed me. I'd done nothing of the sort but of course anything she said he believed.

One of my father's favourite tricks was making me clean the bathroom. That might not sound bad, except that he would lock me in there until I was done. Sometimes he'd go to the pub and forget I was locked in there. I could be left for a whole day, except that his plan had a fatal flaw: the bathroom window led on to the extension roof, and I could just about squeeze through the tiny window, then climb down the side of the guttering and escape. As long as the bathroom was clean and I got back before him it was fine. Well, almost fine.

Firstly, it was not that easy getting back up the extension and through the window, especially when I was trying to do it in a major hurry to avoid being caught. Needless to say I had many falls and injuries as a result of my efforts. Timing could also be a problem because my father was not always predictable. Eventually they either worked out my cunning escape route and couldn't be bothered doing anything about it or just got bored of that punishment as I never kicked up a fuss and they stopped that particular game. I really think that's what they saw it as. Or maybe it's just my survival instinct that led me to look at it that way. I realise I'm quite a strong character: I have always refused to let things get the better of me and don't believe in being a victim, an attitude that has helped me in stripping. Loads of people have dreadful things happen to them, far worse than anything I've gone through. Yes, it was horrible and the most miserable existence but, at the time, it was the only one I knew and I also knew I had to survive it.

Soon I had another problem. I began having stomach pains and they were steadily getting worse. At first I thought it might have been one of the knocks I'd received – I was always tender and bruised – but after a week of it worsening I went to see the school nurse. She wasn't technically a nurse, rather a teacher who knew First Aid, but there was absolutely no way I could go to the doctor or the hospital – it would have sent my father through the roof. So she was my only choice. I told her what was going on and she said it was 'lady pains'. I should have expected something like this: she was the biology teacher who'd almost passed out when she had to say 'condom', and 'lady pains' was just another one of her classics. I was already 15 and had been having my periods for a while so I knew this wasn't that particular type of pain.

I continued in discomfort for about two weeks until one day I was at home and the pain started to become excruciating. I began vomiting and was feeling very hot and weak. Dad was there so I pleaded with him to take me to the hospital but he just got up and went to the pub. Within thirty minutes the situation deteriorated: I broke out in a cold sweat and was feeling faint. I had no other option but to go to the pub for help. Luckily it was only about ten doors away so I literally dragged myself down there – and I mean dragged. I was holding on to fences and walls to support me since I could barely walk. I got to the pub and fell through the door – much to the horror of everyone inside.

Apparently my face had turned green, and I was throwing up everywhere. My dad, playing the loving, caring father, immediately turned on his Father of the Year act for his alcoholic friends. He picked me up and rushed me to the hospital where within forty-five minutes I was in surgery with a burst appendix. Had it been another hour or so, you wouldn't be reading this right now. When I woke up after the surgery Mum was at my bedside, sick with worry.

As for my dad I can only assume he was in the pub telling everyone how he'd saved my life and probably getting bought free beers for his heroic actions! Five days later I was out and everything changed at home. We became a happy family, my mum moved back, my dad stopped drinking and losing his temper and we all lived happily ever after. The end.

Ok, so that didn't happen. But after I got out of hospital my life went back to normal: sitting in the bushes, staying out as much as possible – the usual stuff. Then three months later my life once again flashed before my eyes. One day at school I slipped at the top of the stairs. I hit a wall then fell down the next set of stairs. Since my memory stops at the top step, I can only piece together the rest of the story from what I've been told. Apparently, I landed with my head at the bottom of the stairs and my feet and body twisted up the stairs. I drifted in and out of consciousness until the air ambulance came. It then took them nearly an hour to put me on a backboard (spinal support apparatus) as I was in such an awkward position. When I was stabilised I was then transferred to a normal ambulance and taken to hospital. By the time I got there my mum was already there, standing in the ambulance bay. Apparently she was in a dreadful state and had thought I'd died since the ambulance hadn't arrived at the hospital. I was x-rayed, scanned and given an army of tests. When I did wake up once again it was my mum beside my bed and no dad. Not that I was complaining.

The amazing powers of morphine meant that I could feel very little. Since I was strapped down to the bed I couldn't move any part of me except my eyes. All I knew was that my vision was blurred, but I was in no position to complain.

After what felt like an eternity but was actually about three hours of looking at a blurry hospital ceiling they took off the straps and I could move a small amount. It turned out that I had bruises, bumps and a few cracks – mainly ribs – some damage to my spine (but it wasn't broken) and swelling on the brain, hence the blurry eyesight which led to me needing glasses for seven months. Apart from that it was just heavy bruising, swelling, sprains and strains. A short stay in hospital and I was free to go home.

And what a welcome I received. We had house guests!

While I was in hospital my dad had got himself a new girlfriend, a woman with two kids, and they'd moved in. Secretly I thought he was expecting me to die or be disabled so I wouldn't come back. You might be wondering why he took me back and didn't just throw me out. To all his friends, his pub friends, my father was such a lovely bloke so throwing out his young daughter would have been scandalous, and he wouldn't want anything to damage his reputation. Also, I later found out that my mum was still paying towards the mortgage – he was probably making her pay to have me stay there – so he wouldn't want to lose the steady flow of beer money.

Being the ridiculous optimist that I am, I thought this new situation might work out well and this new woman might mean he'd change his behaviour. Boy, was I wrong. She was a heavy alcoholic. Only a few months previously she'd been in a mental institution and had only just got her kids back part-time. Of course she was homeless and my fool of a father came along. Dad obviously persuaded her what an evil person I was so I had no chance of an ally.

Her presence meant there was a lot more alcohol consumed. In a normal day they easily went through huge amounts of vodka, wine and beer. It was now *her* house and I was no longer free to eat the food in the kitchen. If I was caught eating Dad would punish me – this could range from cleaning the oven, to my head being held as food was forced into my mouth while I gagged and choked. My babysitting money would be taken as soon as I walked in the door. I had no food at home, no money for lunch at school – the only food I had was what my friends shared with me or what I took in desperation from the house where I babysat. You might wonder why I carried on working if they were taking my money as soon as I walked in. Anything was better than being at home, even if my money was taken.

However, things were getting desperate. They would buy fish and chips once a week and I would just watch as they ate them. The bin was in the middle of the kitchen and they'd throw the leftovers away in front of me. This was the worst kind of torture but I was starving so I'd stay up until they all went to bed and then pick the food out of the bin. I'm not sure how, but Dad caught on to this, so the fish and chips ritual took a little change. After throwing the food in the bin Dad would throw cigarette butts and even pee on top of it – anything to stop me eating the bin food.

I was always an incredibly thin child. Before the 'food punishment' started I was a size 6 so now I was literally wasting away. It wasn't hard to see things weren't right but I was too afraid – and ashamed – to tell anyone about my predicament. I thought about telling someone at school but I wanted to fit in and be normal: I hated standing out. I didn't exactly tell Mum but she sensed things were not good so she started bringing me food packages. Either she'd meet me along the road or leave them in my secret bush hiding place. I couldn't tell Mum that if I took it into the house my room would be raided and it would be taken so I would eat as much of the food as soon as she brought it, knowing it would be my only chance. My mum just thought things were uncomfortable, she never had a clue things were any worse. Also my dad had faked her signature on remortgage documents so they were in a serious financial situation;

she slept on the sofa at her work illegally when she could. For a while she was literally living out of her car while she paid the mortgage for my upkeep. I didn't want to add to her burden by telling her how bad things were for me. I just couldn't bring myself to do it.

Most days I'd have little more than a bag of crisps or half a sandwich. Once a week I'd eat at my babysitting job and I'd have my mum's weekly food parcel. At week-ends there was nothing for me to eat, so I'd try to steal from the kitchen but there was always someone in the house. It felt like they even counted the slices of bread.

The newest game was that I got banned from using the washing machine. Even though Mum had bought it I was now told it was out of bounds. I could only hand-wash my uniform at the weekend, but with no soap or washing powder the clothes weren't exactly clean. Everything I owned was in a real state: dirty, tatty and old.

This was far worse than any physical violence. It was a cruel, depraved form of torture. The hunger, the humiliation, the begging, the degradation – nothing at that time could have been worse. I was 15, not mentally strong enough to deal with it but at the same time old enough to be fully aware and understand it. This mental abuse left much deeper scars than any cuts and bruises. At this time my bus money for school also stopped, so I was missing a lot of school, which had been a haven to me. Still no one at school said a word. I would take fake absence notes and gym notes because, not only did I have no kit, I was so undernourished and bruised I was ashamed of my body. (I absolutely hated PE but that was irrelevant in the circumstances.) I had one thing in my life I can look back on and be thankful for. I had a boyfriend who'd just passed his driving test and could sometimes borrow his parents' car. When he could he'd drive me to school, or give me money for the bus. For obvious reasons he never came to mine but on occasion I'd go to his and eat!

One cold morning, about two weeks before my 16th birthday, I was getting ready for school and begging my dad for bus money when he grabbed me by the hair and threw me across the room. As I got up I felt something sharp and hard in my back and crumpled to the floor in agony. I was shocked. He knew I'd only got out of hospital less than three months ago, where I had been treated for damage to my spine, and he had hit me in the back. I was so angry, I got up, turned around and screamed at him, 'I can't believe you hit me in the back!'

He laughed and said, 'I didn't hit you, I kicked you.' That was the last straw. As he tried to grab me again, I ran out of the house and down the road to the phone box. He didn't follow me and I knew he was too lazy to do so. I called my boyfriend by reverse charges and 15 minutes later he came and picked me up. I was huddled in the phone box, crying and shaking. It was mid-November and I was barefoot and wearing only my school trousers and a crop top. I was bleeding and could barely stand, partly because of the cold but mainly due to the pain in my back. My boyfriend was horrified: he drove me to school and got a teacher. I can't really recall what happened for the rest of that day; I suppose a mixture of shock and relief took over. I remember teachers looking at me almost in tears, as they saw the cuts and bruises and how emaciated I was. I had to repeat the events of that morning over and over, but by now I was on autopilot. Everyone assumed it was a one-off incident but they were still shocked. They took photographs and called my mum.

When all was said and done they had to find me somewhere to live. As I was now 16, a help group took me on; it was a combination of a child welfare government agency and a charity to help youngsters find refuge and help them get government support, jobs etc. Basically it bridged that gap for kids like me who were too old for help but too young for life.

For the first few weeks my boyfriend's parents took me in. It was against everything they believed as they were deeply religious but they were more than happy to help and it was either that or a short-term hostel, home of drug addicts and ex-convicts. My time here was amazing: I ate, watched TV – something I had only ever done when babysitting – and lived normally while my housing situation was being arranged.

I was soon given my own flat in a block for 'troubled youngsters'. I was ecstatic: my own flat and everyone would be like me. Plus it was long-term so I wouldn't have to move. The building was newly decorated so it was all clean and fresh. I had my own bathroom and kitchen – what more did I need? It was in an area I hardly knew and very far from my school, but at the time I didn't care. It was the happiest day I'd had since I could remember. I had no bed, no furniture, nothing – but I was so happy. I kept my food out on the windowsill as I had no fridge. I was given some vouchers for a charity shop where I bought a mattress, a cupboard, a mirror, some shoes and clothes and eventually a fridge.

My mum bought me a sofa, quilt, sheets, plates and all the other little bits and bobs to make it a home. I remember her taking me to Ikea to buy some stuff and we saw a sofa in the bargain corner for next to nothing. She bought it for me not realising we had to take it then and there, so we ended up sat outside Ikea for several hours on the sofa while we waited for David, her new partner, to come and pick us up in his van. It was one of my happiest memories, sitting on my new sofa being a mother and daughter and eating hot dogs, until a guy in a full dress suit (he managed a very posh restaurant) got out of a beat-up VW to lug the sofa into the van and take me home.

Every week Mum would take me shopping to the supermarket to buy my food. I was still going to school every day and I'd still managed to get good grades in my GCSEs so was now doing my A-levels. I was given twenty pounds a week from the government which didn't quite pay for my travel to school and lunch but I had a part-time job. I bought a cheap CD player, clothes, chocolate – normal teenage things. For the first time in my life I could live as a normal teenager. Life was tough but it was better than it had been.

Chapter 10

❦

Down but never out

Living in the flat at 16 meant I learned to be independent very early on. It was an experience that shaped me in many ways and, thinking back, it probably prepared me to cope with the emotional and mental demands of being a stripper. It wasn't an easy life trying to look after myself and going to school, but I'm not someone who sits around moaning. It was the life I had and it taught me a hell of a lot about surviving in the real world.

I remember being really happy when I moved in to my own place – it seemed the best solution to the problems with my father and I could get on with my studies. I didn't know that the area I was living in was very bad; there was high crime and drug abuse. I was only the second tenant to move in to the block of six flats but by the end of the week the building was nearly full. Being naïve and young I thought all the 'troubled' teenagers would be like me – not so troubled. Wrong. The flats were filled with young girls who seemed to have more than their fair share of drug and alcohol problems. No one knew what to do with them so they were placed there. I wasn't prepared for what I saw. There were used needles outside my door, men of all sorts and ages going up and down the stairs and 'boyfriends' of the girls passed out in the hallways.

Within a week the communal door had been smashed in, and within two weeks my front door had been broken down and I'd been burgled. This happened pretty regularly. Once they'd taken the valuables, they'd steal the food out of my cupboards. My door was broken down so regularly the wooden frame was destroyed and you only had to lean on it to open it. I called the police; they took a statement and said they would send someone to fix the door at my expense – I couldn't afford it, so that never happened. Mum came round and we actually nailed and screwed the door frame as best we could but that only lasted so long.

My new flat was about 15 miles from my school and even further from my friends so I saw them less and less. We were all so wrapped up in our A-levels anyway. The distance became too difficult and eventually I stopped seeing my boyfriend. It was costing me £3.50

to get to school each day. I was being given £20 a week to live on from the government. You do the maths. I tried to appeal for further help, saying I could barely pay my travel, let alone eat and pay my bills, but I was told to change schools. As far as I was concerned there was no way I was leaving my good school to go to one in the area I lived in.

I took on two jobs to be able to afford to travel to school and eat. That meant working three or four nights a week, going to school all day and doing a different job at the weekend. This was before the establishment of the minimum wage, so I was earning next to nothing, but it was better than nothing. I was knackered. I was working constantly, was being robbed regularly, had no friends, no boyfriend, no family (Mum was still trying to sort her situation out), no money, no time and no freedom. My health wasn't so good since I wasn't eating or sleeping properly. My flat was opposite a Chinese takeaway and the owners lived in the flat above. They must have noticed me leaving in my school uniform at 6am and coming back about midnight in work clothes. If I made it home before midnight, I would stop at the Chinese and order whatever I could afford – usually boiled rice and barbecue sauce, the most filling and cheapest thing on the menu. I would literally count out my pennies for the food or ask if I could leave an IOU for 50p or however much I was short. After a month or two if I didn't make it back before closing, they would sometimes leave leftovers on the front ledge of the shop for me for free. I don't know if they felt sorry for me or realised my desperate situation – probably both. But I would happily take this food and devour it. They did this about once a week. At the time it was the only act of kindness anyone did for me and I will never forget it.

Not surprisingly I was exhausted and miserable. I would sometimes spend all day in the dark crying and vomiting. Sometimes, I would curl up in the corner and not move for several hours. Once a boy broke through my door and burgled me – what little I had – while I was sat in the corner, silent and not moving. The reason I didn't move wasn't because I was scared: I didn't care and had very little fear left. I just physically couldn't move. He never even knew I was there. I sat and watched him steal half a pint of milk and two cans of beans. There was nothing else to take.

I was so incredibly lonely and felt rejected by everyone. I was missing lots of school because I had no choice but to work and took an extra job working behind a bar. It was illegal since I was only just 17. My life was pretty much about working and going to school when I could. Luckily I was pretty strong academically as even though my grades were starting to slip, I was still hanging in there. There was a guy working in the bar who took a shine to me. He was 29 and I thought he was charming. He treated me well and spoke to me like a person and I felt good. He did his best to chat me up but I never gave in to his advances. I can't tell you why, whether it was lack of self-confidence, lack of trust in men, or just me being me.

One night, around midnight, I was walking home from work when I was aware of someone following me. I was only about fifty steps from my front door, so I hurried. By the time I had my key in the door, he was right behind me. I had the door open but my keys were still in the lock. I hurried through the door but was still trying to fumble with the keys. I closed the door as much as I could, so it was between him and me: all I kept thinking was 'Don't let go of the keys.' He'd grabbed my arm which was still holding the keys in his side of the door and I knew I had to react as there was no way I had the strength to hold him off.

I slammed the front door on his arm, which was holding my arm. I did this about a dozen times, each time slamming my own hand and arm in the door as well. Eventually he let go. I shut the door and locked myself in the bathroom. My front door was unsafe and the only secure door was the bathroom. My arm was a mess: there was hardly any skin along my forearm, blood everywhere and my hand was a swollen blob. My face was red and swollen and starting to bruise and my mouth was bleeding. I dared not report it to the police. One, I had no phone and couldn't face leaving the building and two, I'd recognised the man; he was a local guy who came into the pub I worked at, a notorious criminal, only about 20 years old but famed in the area for being dangerous. He'd made a fair few lewd comments my way but I'd always rejected his advances – the last thing I wanted in my life was another temperamental, violent and disturbed man after escaping my dad's clutches!

I cleaned myself up, and sat in the bathroom, scared to leave until it got light. I went back to work two days later, bruised and battered. I just told people I had been attacked. The charming guy was shocked: he told the boss to send me home but I refused, saying I needed the money. The guy gave me what I would've earned in my shift and told me to go home. 'Wow,' I thought, 'what an amazing guy!' I went back to school a few days later, but I was so embarrassed about the state of my uniform and bag. I felt humiliated. One night at work I was feeling so low about this, so ashamed of myself, I suppose I thought I couldn't get any lower, so I stole £20 out of the till. I remember that even while doing it I knew it wasn't right but I needed stupid things like tights, shampoo and a new shirt, and just couldn't afford them. Two days later I got sacked.

Once again the charming guy was there to be nice to me and reassure me, so the charming guy soon became my boyfriend. He paid me the attention that I so desperately needed. He complimented me, smiled at me and hugged me. These simple things were worth a lot to me right then. He had my door fixed and some strong bolts put on it. He was the first man ever to give me a sense of safety. He bought me presents, clothes and furniture and he took me out. These first few months of our relationship were an incredible time for me. I went from looking like an anorexic charity shop reject to a fairly healthy young woman. I gained about a stone, got the colour back in my skin and even started to smile again. I sat my A-level exams, which I astonishingly passed, and I got a full-time job working in an office in a car garage. I would go clubbing, get drunk and be a teenager again. What I didn't realise – but I'm sure he did – was that I was totally dependent on him, this charming boyfriend. I felt he had saved my life. Meanwhile he was playing mind games with me, making me think that I needed him and couldn't live without him. By the time I was 17, I wasn't just hooked on him, I was almost hooked on drugs.

I don't actually remember the first time I took drugs. I think my boyfriend may have been giving them to me gradually without me really knowing. I would get drunk often and it wouldn't have been hard. I'd taken Ecstasy before when I was 15 and at the occasional rave but this was different. I was taking coke two or three times a week and eventually nearly every day. I was totally under his control. His charming act had dropped and I now realised he was actually a drug dealer, who was sometimes aggressive. He would hide drugs at my house and have people coming and going at all times. His sleazy addict friends would come knocking at the door day and night and sometimes stay for hours. If I ever complained, he would tell me how useless and damaged I was and that I was lucky to have someone like him as no one else would want me. I believed him and would not complain again. Except for the visitors it wasn't too bad because it was the only life I knew.

I was taking drugs and drinking most nights and the people I classed as friends were all criminals and drug users so my lifestyle didn't seem out of the ordinary at the time. This also had the effect of me not realising how much of a hold he had over me. I soon became slightly scared of him but at the same time I was scared to lose him. He would disappear for days and not explain where he'd been. Or he would have his friends round to my flat smoking crack and there was nothing I could say because he would just humiliate me in front of them. And then it would be all fun again: we'd go to all the top clubs in London, drink champagne, and have a great time. I had more friends – well, I knew more people – than I ever had, and I knew that while I was with him, no one would harm me. That was something. Unfortunately the bad times quickly outnumbered the good and I soon lost my job. His reputation was known and the car company didn't want me to go out with him. That was rather ironic considering they bought and sold dodgy cars, but I was now without a job.

My boyfriend told me his friend was a model and he would have a word and get me in with the agent. I was amazed, I never dreamed I could do that but the fact that he suggested it made me feel great. One day he came to my house and said the agent wanted to meet me, so he took me along to see this guy who took some pictures of me in my underwear as well as topless. Within weeks I was doing a paid photoshoot. I was getting paid about £50 to £70 for half a day's work, which at the time I thought was fantastic. All I had to do was stand there in sexy underwear. I have no idea what the shoots were for but I was so young and naïve and just too happy to be actually getting modelling work to ask questions.

After a few shoots I felt like a professional. One day my agent called me in to see him. I went to see him with my boyfriend and he basically said I wasn't good enough to do the topless shots but he had a few nude shoots I could do. I didn't realise this was his slimy way of getting me to pose totally nude. He told me if I improved he could get me some high-profile glamour shoots for the *Sun*, *Loaded* etc. But only if I did these shoots, so I could get better at it. He really made it sound like he could make me a star and make all my wildest dreams come true – if I just did these nude shots first. I really wasn't keen but they talked me into it. My boyfriend's attitude was basically, 'I got you this opportunity and you're throwing it back in my face.' He'd say this in the most angry threatening way and then he'd hug me and kiss me. He knew exactly how to manipulate me. I agreed to do it.

The first shoot actually turned out to be soft porn. My boyfriend drove me there telling me he loved me and no one else would. In a numb state, I posed naked for this horrible little photographer, got paid and was driven home. It was nothing too explicit but it was bad enough. I did this for a few months, travelling around the country doing a few shots a week. I'd just turned 18 so was barely legal which, funnily enough, was also the title of one of the magazines I worked for. I was earning good money, working a lot and even though I felt like shit, I was gaining a bit of confidence, even though it was in the wrong way.

I worked with other girls who happily did their job. Doing these shoots made me believe I had something wrong with me. So much had happened in my life, I was starting to think it must be my fault and that I must be a bad or horrible person for this to happen. I thought maybe I didn't deserve to be happy, so I would bottle up my sadness and discomfort and carry on working when I should have just left. I tried to be good at my job and wanted people to like me. I did some TV stuff for a Sky porn channel and would go home thoroughly disgraced, feeling like I needed to scrub my skin, and that I didn't deserve better. I suppose I was lucky in that I didn't get involved in hardcore porn. My agent promised there was better work coming up and I hung on for dear life hoping I would never have to pose like this again.

One day I met a girl, Emily, who was tall, striking, well dressed and strong. I admired her so much. She would come to buy crack and cocaine off my boyfriend as she was an addict, but at the time I could only see this beautiful, strong woman. We'd speak a lot and I became friends with her. One day she told me my boyfriend was constantly cheating on me (it was true) and that he had a child with his ex and one of his other girlfriends was pregnant (also true). This was a massive wake-up call. Meanwhile Emily told me I didn't need to do the soft porn. She worked as a stripper and loved her job, earned loads of money and thought that I could easily get a job. I wasn't sure. In any case I wanted to give up the 'modelling'. So I quit.

I confronted my boyfriend about his other girlfriends. We had a massive row; I stood my ground and he left. The next day I was badly beaten up in the street by two girls, which I knew wasn't just coincidence. They tore out my hair, split my eye open, broke a tooth, kicked me all over and spat on me. The only thing I could do was curl up in a ball on the street until they ran off. I just lay there hoping that it wouldn't last long and since it was broad daylight there was a chance they'd soon be disturbed. Luckily they bolted when they saw people coming. About four days later, he turned up at my flat. It was late at night. I woke up, went in the kitchen and saw him hiding a gun behind the plinth under the kitchen cabinets. I froze but had to think quickly.

I said nothing that night and the next morning asked him to get rid of the gun, which he did. While he was out I got an emergency locksmith to change the locks and I put all his stuff in black sacks outside the front door. I then searched the flat for any hidden drugs – which I found – and flushed them down the toilet. I sat at home for the rest of the day expecting trouble, but I wasn't scared – I think my sense of fear left me a long time ago – but trouble never came, until a few days later when my flat was raided by police. Of course they found nothing as I had scoured the flat and got rid of his stash. I'm sure he tipped off the police thinking I wouldn't have had the sense to remove the drugs, but he underestimated me. I suppose I was lucky in that I wasn't personally addicted to the drugs. Sure, I took them while they were there but I never really yearned for them or craved them after this episode. It was as if I'd shut the door on it all.

I was still friends with Emily and we would go out to parties. She'd never let me pay for anything and would always lend me clothes. I was kind of like a little sister to her and it was fun. I saw how good her life was: she earned great money, had a nice flat and – best of all – ran her own life on her terms. But sadly she was a drug user and I'd stopped taking drugs the day that guy left my life. So I stopped seeing her but took her advice and decided to go for an audition as a dancer. And that's how I ended up at Stringfellows. Depending on which way you look at it, it was as simple or as complicated as that.

Chapter 11

No not that hair, THAT hair

After I'd left Strings, it dawned on me how very few real friends I had. The girls I'd met while dancing were mostly too busy with work and their own lives, so we ended up losing touch. It's to be expected really: the stripping world is a bubble and once you step outside of it you don't really exist to those people any more. New girls start, things change and people forget you. When you're stripping you're so absorbed in your job you have little time for outside friends. Even Tamara and I found it hard to get together often since she was still working at Strings and had little free time.

The girls I met while modelling for the lads' magazines were even more superficial. If you weren't out in the clubs acting like a superstar – as they were – they didn't want to know you. At the same time there was loads of backstabbing between girls to get the plum jobs so you couldn't really trust anyone. I was still getting a modelling job at least once a week, and while it was good for recognition and boosted my self-esteem, it didn't offer big financial rewards. A glamour model like Jordan is the exception in terms of earning money this way, but she is an extreme in every sense! The bulk of glamour modelling, which takes in Page Three of the *Sun* and the popular magazines like *Loaded*, paid really badly in comparison to what I'd been used to earning at Strings. I'd been so used to making seriously good money I started to feel the difference very quickly.

Seeing as I had no interest in finding myself a celebrity/footballer boyfriend I figured that I was much better suited to dancing and had little choice but to go back there. My first port of call was the library, where there were computers, so I could browse the internet for London clubs. There was no way I was going back to Strings; there were too many bitchy girls there now and I just couldn't go back to working that hard and risk wearing myself down again. I felt that a fresh start was in order.

I decided on a club in Soho. I auditioned – which was much less nerve-racking than it'd been the first time – and started that same night. Boy, did I get a shock. I guess I was used to the relative civility of Strings and this club was miles away from that. It wasn't in the same league as Strings – the girls weren't as attractive and with these low standards came a general feeling of low morale and a lot of tension among the strippers. I saw just how nasty the girls were when I started attracting lots of customers that night. There were actually very few customers and being the new girl in a room full of girls who weren't that good meant that I was doing rather well.

The other girls didn't like it. And what's more they weren't going to sit back and watch. Within an hour and a half of starting my shift there, one girl 'accidentally' spilled a glass of red wine all over me. When I went to change, one of my outfits was missing while the other had makeup smeared all over it. My hair straighteners were switched on and a plastic bag had been wrapped round them so the plastic had melted on to the plates, which meant they were now ruined. I found my makeup bag and realised it was my makeup they'd used to smear all over my dress. I'd never experienced anything like this at Strings and suddenly felt very alone. I spoke to the House Mum, who was obviously friends with the hyenas: she just shrugged and wasn't interested. So I asked to see the manager who'd auditioned me but he'd left.

Seeing as I now had not a single outfit to wear and couldn't wait to get out of that disgusting place, I decided to quit. But it wasn't that easy. The House Mum said I had to pay my house fee of £60 before I left – even though the manager had told me I only had to pay half as it was my first night. Naturally I refused as I'd worked less than two hours and also had all of my belongings destroyed. That's when it got heavy. Really heavy and really scary. The House Mum told me that if I didn't give her £60 then she would have the bouncers beat me up. I was terrified and just wanted to get out of that place as quickly as possible. I was trembling as I took out my purse with the money I'd earned so far that night, as well as my own money. Before I could do anything she snatched the purse away from me. She then took all the money out of my purse and called the bouncers to throw me out, telling them she'd caught me stealing. These two burly guys walked in, picked me up and threw me into the street like a piece of meat. Everyone just looked at me as I picked myself up, humiliated. I couldn't believe what had happened. I took the train home in tears and after that adventure, didn't even think of dancing for a few months. That still left me with the problem of what to do with myself.

*

A little while later I met up with a few girls I'd worked with at Strings. It was good to be with people who'd shared the same experiences. One of the girls, Angie, had left there before I had. She was now working in another club and really enjoying it so suggested I should come down, have a drink and maybe audition. She said the money was good and also that she worked shorter shifts than she'd done at Strings and still made more money. This sounded too good to be true so I went there one night to check it out.

So one cold, wintry evening in January, I headed down to this place in East London. Angie was working that night and told me to come along for a drink and just check the place out. This isn't usually the norm; girls tend not to go into clubs unless auditioning or working, but she said it was different there. As it turned out it *was* too good to be true: it wasn't a club at all, but a pub, a pub with strippers. My eyes had suddenly been opened to the darker world of stripping. From the moment I walked into this cavernous building with its dark doors and muted exterior, to the traditional pub interior (this was no modern pub conversion) with its grey walls and dodgy patterned carpet, I was rudely awakened to the stark realisation that stripping wasn't just high-profile clubs with opulent interiors and rich clientele. It was a shock, and a rather big one, to find myself in what was essentially a pub that was only frequented by men.

I walked into this large room with its bland interior and long bar where men were standing around drinking pints and eating crisps. Just as I was thinking of making a run for it, I saw Angie heading towards me from the back of the room. She gave me a hug and I knew I couldn't back out now. I followed her back to the table where she sat with a few other girls. She went to the bar to get me a drink – I was way too embarrassed to go up there myself – while I took a seat on a little moth-eaten pub stool at the back of this vast, mostly empty room. I watched a girl on stage. She was dancing and then it suddenly dawned on me: she was doing it totally naked. I sat slightly stunned and incredibly embarrassed until Angie came back with my Diet Coke, laughed at my clearly disturbed facial expression and told me, yes, they did dance naked here. She went on to tell me more about the club, how easy the job was and that I would really enjoy working there. I met a few other girls and I have to admit they all seemed friendly, and seemed to be having a good laugh doing it. There was a really nice girl called Crystal who spoke to me and supported Angie's positive views about the pub/club but I'd already decided: no way.

Over the next few weeks, I went out with Angie a few

times partly because it was good to have someone to talk to. I usually met her before or after work for a drink and she was so happy; she'd tell me how much she'd earned, even though it was January, traditionally the quietest time of the year for stripping. Slowly but surely she was convincing me that I should give it a go. I just couldn't get over the fact that the girls danced naked, let alone that it took place in a pub. But after going out with her a few times, I thought 'what the hell'.

I called the office the next morning and arranged to go in for an interview. Now in most places you'll turn up on an appointed day and do an audition, but here you had to have an interview first where they took your details and a topless photo. If they liked that then you were given an audition. So I headed down there and through to the office at the back, where a woman asked me a few questions about my age, where I'd worked before and how long I'd been working. I told her I'd been 'Best New Angel' at Strings, something I was then still quite proud of, and I showed her the modelling photo I'd brought with me in case the picture they took of me was no good. She didn't seem too interested and then went on to take a topless picture of me using a cheap Polaroid camera, which made me look the same colour as the magnolia wall behind me. They'd be in touch.

A few days later, on Valentine's Day, I got a call from

the woman saying they were short of girls and was it possible I could start that night. I wasn't sure so asked the woman if I could start another day as I really needed time to prepare. She wasn't too impressed with my response and told me that if I turned that shift down, it would look really bad and I might not get any more shifts. So I had no choice but to turn up that evening. She started to tell me what I needed to bring with me. For a crappy pub they seemed to want you to make a lot more effort than Strings: I had to bring five or six different outfits as well as my own music.

As soon as I'd hung up the phone I panicked. Five or six different outfits! I rummaged through all my old costumes to see what might be suitable. It'd been at least six months since I'd danced and seeing as a few of my best costumes had been ruined at my last horrendous attempt at dancing I had very little left. And as for bringing my own music, at Strings, you had to dance to whatever song you were unfortunate enough to get so I had to suddenly find music to get up on stage to. What I thought would be just another dancing job was turning out to be a totally different ball game. On top of that I was desperately trying not to think about the fact that I would be getting up on stage and stripping down to absolutely nothing, no knickers, nothing. This brought about another train of thought. If I was going to be knickerless in front of a roomful of men, what should I ... what should my pubic area look like?

I remember having a bath, doing the usual ritual of shaving legs and underarms, and then I looked at my bikini area and thought, 'What the hell do I do with that?' as if it were some sort of strange animal that had landed on my doorstep. This was before the days of Brazilian waxing, before shapes, patterns, dyes and diamantes were topics of conversation in the pub. You couldn't walk into your local salon and ask for a Hollywood (everything off); they'd send you to the travel agents. I was so worried at the thought of getting up on stage and looking like a fool in front of the other girls, who were sure to know things I didn't. What if there was a certain 'look'? I decided to phone Angie.

'Hi Angela, I'm a bit worried about this naked thing. I mean what exactly am I supposed to do with my ... you know ... pubic hair.'

'What are you on about? Just do what you usually do!'

'Well I've never *had* to do anything, I've never done the full monty before, should I shave it or trim it? I mean, I don't know, is there a shape everyone's into right now? I'm just a bit worried I might get it wrong.'

I know it might sound bizarre but, trust me, if you had to get on a stage, naked, in front of a roomful of men, you would be thinking about this too. It's different now; you can go to pretty much any beauty salon and have your pubes shaped into red hearts. I must've sounded pretty desperate but when she stopped laughing she told me not to panic.

'Get *what* wrong? Just shave your bits and keep them tidy. It'll be fine.'

No, there was no particular look. I should just do what I thought looked good, whatever that was. I continued with my bath. Here I am, I thought. About to embark on another crazy, last-minute, unprepared, not-fully-thought-through misadventure. I remember getting a cab as the rain was pelting down and I'd just spent the last hour doing my hair and makeup, so I treated myself. Normally I'd never spend money on a cab unless I was coming home late; to me it was just a huge waste of money. Thirty minutes and twenty quid later I stood ready to face my awaiting public, and to make my naked debut on stage.

I got there early. I was supposed to be there at eight to start at 8.30 but Angie was working on the shift before, so she suggested I come in early and have a drink or six, which is exactly what I did. She wasn't around when I walked in so I went to the bar, told them it was my first day and they sent me through a little door to change. As I walked through the bar I glanced at the stage and there was Angie. I didn't realise it was her at first as the bits I was seeing I certainly hadn't seen before. Slightly embarrassed, I just kept my head down and headed for the changing room.

The room itself was accessed through a door beside the stage. It wasn't really a room; it was no bigger than a generous closet and smelled of sweaty shoes, old smoke and cheap perfume. To the right was a hanging rail holding what I guessed must be lost property and things left behind. These ranged from men's coats, bags and umbrellas to a Viking helmet; crumpled costumes including a toga; bags, wigs and a lasso which I could only hope belonged to one of the girls. To the left of me were two dirty mirrors covered in old notices, the remainders of stickers and makeup. There were two threadbare bar stools and piles of bags, clothes, shoes and costumes scattered over the filthy lino. Among this pile of crap – because what else could you call it – I found a relatively dirt- and mess-free place for my bag and me. Standing underneath the harsh unflattering light I looked around me. 'What the hell am I getting into?' I asked myself, wishing I was at home.

Once again, Angie was there to rescue me. Fresh off stage and out of breath, she made a timely entrance to pull me out of the self-pity I was starting to slip in to.

'Hi babes. It's great to see you.'

Sensing my concern she took me under her wing. 'Look, you've got ages before your shift so there's plenty of time to have a drink and calm down. Have you put your name down on the rota yet?'

'No, not yet.'

'OK, I'll just get changed and then we'll go and get you organised. Don't worry.'

Yep, I was worried.

Once she'd quickly changed into the world's shortest black PVC zip-front dress and applied yet another layer of lip gloss and perfume, we headed out to the bar.

I may have been dancing for a few years, but I was a total fish out of water here. Everything was different. For starters, the pub was open from midday to midnight, or 1am depending of the night of the week. Being open for such long hours meant they split this into three shifts which were imaginatively called the lunch shift, the middle shift and the late shift. The lunch was from 12 till 5, the middle 5 till 8.30/9 and the late until 12/1. From Monday to Wednesday the pub closed at midnight, the rest of the week 1am. When I arrived, Angie was on the middle shift and I was to be on the late one. Coming into your shift at this place meant putting your name on a list behind the bar: this list determines the order in which you go on stage. On a late shift, everyone battles to get there early to be first as you earn more money that way, so even though I was there over an hour before my shift started, I was already number five. As it was a Thursday there were eight girls working that night. It was all very different to the seventy-odd girls they'd have on any night at Strings. The number of girls working was dependent on what day it was and what shift you were on. A typical Monday lunch shift, for example, would have four girls working and a Friday late would have ten.

So I followed orders and put my name on the list and there was already a welcome glass of wine waiting for me on the bar. I followed Angie to the back of the room where we sat with a huddle of girls, some working that shift, others waiting to do the next one with me. It was pretty relaxed here in terms of not having the kind of rules I was used to at Strings. You could drink in the bar in your civvies, have friends come in, and the atmosphere among the girls seemed pretty good. My past experiences had left me with the view that I should keep my distance as everyone is out for themselves, so I didn't speak to too many people, just absorbed my surroundings.

The club was a vast room with high ceilings and a really empty feeling; because it was Valentine's Day it was particularly quiet and I'd say there were no more than fifteen guys, which made it feel even more chilly and cavernous. The prison-grey walls, horrid pub carpet covered in cigarette burns and the dim lighting made it feel seedy. Halfway down the room was the largest, most unflatteringly lit stage I had ever seen. It had two poles and a mirror all along the back and was raised off the ground to about elbow height, which gave the men at the front a bird's eye view of proceedings. There was the usual bar selling sandwiches and crisps. And beyond the stage was a curtained-off area with several poles on mini platforms for private dancing with seating all around, cheap plastic plants and, of course, more mirrors.

The anxiety really hit me when Angie began to run through the mechanics of how it all worked. Before you went on stage you had to go around the pub with a pint jug – literally an old-fashioned, heavy glass pint jug – and every customer had to put a pound in. This sounded so awful – it just seemed so horrifying, degrading and humiliating and I was so thankful that there were only a handful of customers there. When you weren't on stage or collecting ('doing the jug') you could work the room trying to get private dances. I took this all in, watching a girl called Coco doing her collection with a fixed grin on her face. Watching, slightly embarrassed, the girls stark naked on stage leaving nothing to the imagination. One particular girl was on stage, legs in the air, showing what she had for breakfast, when Angie, who must have been reading my face, told me I didn't have to expose myself quite so pornographically. But how not to?

She told me to watch her next dance and copy that, as she did some moves that protected her dignity a little more than the girl on stage. In any case, she said, just showing a glimpse of the goods can be much more provocative than being spread upside down on a pole showing what God gave you, and then some. This was reassuring as seeing the other girls perform had absolutely terrified me. So, after another glass of wine while I studied Angie's dance (in which she actually did a sexy dance instead of just spreading her legs) I was ready to get changed and face the music. I had ten minutes before my shift started so I put on my first costume, a purple sparkly asymmetric skirt and matching boob tube, a little moisturiser, topped up my lip gloss and was ready to go. There was still a little time before it was my turn to 'do the jug' and go on stage and I didn't yet have the guts to ask someone if they wanted a private dance so I sat with Angie – she was kindly staying for my shift – and we got pissed. That was going to be the only way I could do it. As there were very few customers and they were mostly regulars, I had quite a few drinks sent over, with me being the nervous new girl and all.

By the time it was my turn to collect it was thankfully still quite empty with not even twenty guys there. I picked up my pint jug from the bar and started my collection – one good thing about this was it had taken my mind off actually going on stage. So after intensive instruction and guidance from Angie, I approached the first guy. The good thing was you didn't have to actually ask for a pound; they knew the drill so it didn't feel as much like begging as I first thought it would. You literally approach the guy holding the jug and smile, or say, 'I'm up next.' It really was that simple. I effortlessly did my first jug, with no problems, stress or major fuck-ups. Now I just had to face my first naked stage show.

Because it was so quiet that night, my jug took just a few minutes. A few men stopped me to ask if I was new, when did I start and my name, but mainly it was a quick walk around. With just over five minutes until I was to go on, I went to the toilet for about the tenth time, and got my CDs ready so I was all set. When I was finally called by the DJ he turned out to be a grumpy little guy who sat in a booth next to the stage and didn't acknowledge me, save for taking my music. I really felt like it was my first time on stage as everything was so different. The size of the stage and the fact that I was about to be stark naked were my main worries, but at least I had actually learned to dance and I didn't have to worry about tripping over my dress and falling flat on my face (even though that was still a possibility).

It was over pretty quickly and I think I managed well even though the boss told me afterwards that I could not take my knickers off in the last ten seconds: it had to be a bit sooner. Well, you have to see what you can get away with, don't you? I actually felt fine, not degraded or objectified in any way. The people were nice, even though there were three guys stood directly at the front of the stage an arm's length away focusing intently on my pubic area. In actual fact I didn't feel I'd overstepped the line in any way, and the fact that I was naked didn't feel overly uncomfortable or embarrassing, but then again, I was very pissed. As soon as I came off stage I was approached by a guy for a dance and I was off; my new career as a stripper at Diamonds had begun. (I should also tell you that this club wasn't called Diamonds. For safety reasons – my own – I've had to change the names of the pubs and the people who worked there.)

During the course of that night I had to go on stage five times, each time collecting in my jug when the girl before me was on stage. It sounds simple enough, but when you're changing, doing private dances and generally just not concentrating it's easily missed. I was late once or twice, but because I was new and it was a quiet night, I was let off. Usually if you're late the DJ has a tantrum. You had to remember all this and also change costumes between each of your stage shows. Hence the need to have five outfits a night. I'd just about managed to scrape together five half-decent outfits. Even though it hadn't been a long time since I'd left Strings my taste had changed considerably and my previous outfits looked tatty and old.

I earned £150 that night, which was excellent, as it was deathly quiet and it was my first night. Like Angie said, it really was easy money. There were no high house fees to worry about – your jug would always more than cover that. You didn't have seventy other girls to battle with and the money was there for the taking, hassle free. You'd keep your jug of coins with you all night, and after your last show on stage you'd count them out behind the bar, give the club a small percentage and then keep the rest. As well as keeping most of your jug money, you got to keep all of your private dance money. I went home that night quite happy and woke up the next morning with a huge hangover. But I felt good and was actually looking forward to my next shift.

That morning I phoned the office as I was told, to see if there were more shifts for me. Again this is where Diamonds was totally different from anywhere else I had ever been or heard of. Firstly, on a Monday, you had to phone in the morning and tell them when you were available to work the following week, and every day you had a shift you had to phone that same morning between ten and twelve to confirm the booking. It was quite strict: if you forgot or missed calling in by even five minutes, your shift was taken away, as was the shift for the next day. If you did this too often you were fired. This was simple enough and I had my alarm set on my phone so that I very rarely missed it; however there were girls who found it a problem, especially after a big night out. That morning I phoned and the lady in the office said that I would be on cancellations for now and that on Monday when I gave my availability I would get proper shifts. Meanwhile she had a cancellation for Monday. It was at one of their other clubs. I was slightly caught off guard as I had no idea that they had other places, but she told me it was just a smaller version of Diamonds. Apparently all the girls had to work at least two venues.

Chapter 12

❧

Pearls before swine

With the weekend came some much-needed relaxation and the opportunity to buy myself some new costumes, as the five per shift rule was non-negotiable and you couldn't wear the same ones over and over. This left me short of options so I headed off excitedly to Ann Summers. I loved shopping there; they always had new things and didn't charge the earth yet you could look really good. I'd bought a pink babydoll from there when I first started at Strings but it had long since gone to that place where tatty, discoloured lingerie should go (take note girls, there is nothing worse than lingerie that has seen better days).

Shopping for new outfits was a real treat since I was very careful about money and saw no need to spend unnecessarily. On the other hand, spending money in order to make money made good business sense. It also made me feel great. I went into the shop and saw loads of things I wanted but the one that really caught my eye was a black fitted babydoll with pink ribbon trim on the bra cup. It was incredibly short and would make my legs look longer. I absolutely loved it and it was by far the nicest thing I'd ever bought in terms of lingerie. I wanted – and needed – to buy so much more but as I'd put myself on a budget until I got my earnings up to a high level, I held back. It was, however, the start of what was to become a wardrobe of sexy outfits.

I was all set for Monday. This other pub – let's call it Pearls – was a bit further into the City. After calling to confirm, I was ready to set off. I had a bag of costumes, stripper shoes, CDs, makeup and the address. I headed into East London on the tube and emerged at Old Street station twenty minutes later. I knew the club was out of walking distance and had no idea of the direction so I jumped in a cab. Luckily the driver knew straight away where I meant. The traffic was horrendous and even though it was only five minutes' drive away, I ended up arriving late. There was a manager there who didn't seem very nice – much like the girls, they alternated between the clubs – and it was my bad luck to land him on my first day.

'You're late,' he barked.

'Well, yes, I'm sorry … but the traffic –'

He wasn't interested. 'Hurry up and get changed. If you're not on that floor in five minutes I'll fine you.'

I had no idea where the changing rooms were and where I had to put my name on the list so I tried to ask him but he shouted and turned to serve a customer. Luckily one of the barmaids pointed to a door behind the bar and I ran through and got changed in record time. It was not a good start. I went out on to the floor as ordered, and luckily there was a girl that I'd worked with at the other place. She told me where to put my name down, got me a jug and showed me round. As bad as I thought Diamonds was, this place was worse. It was a dump; the only good thing was that the changing rooms were bigger and cleaner. The venue itself was a normal, rough-looking pub, painted in unremarkable shades of brown with a downtrodden, green patterned carpet and an old-fashioned wooden bar. There were fruit machines and a shabby set of old leather bench-style sofas for the girls to sit on between shows. It was all pretty dismal.

The stage wasn't that large but what made it worse was that it was quite low, almost like you were in the crowd. There was one pole and, once again, the infamous mirrored wall at the back and the DJ booth to the side. And much like Diamonds, there was a curtained area with podiums and poles for private dancing. It was a middle shift on a Monday so it wasn't very busy; there were only five or six guys there. With nothing better to do I sat on the unhappy-looking sofa and looked around wishing I was anywhere but there. The walls were scuffed and had paper peeling off them, the carpet was covered in burns and was worn down in many places. There was a disgusting smell of old smoke lingering in the air and it was freezing. Apart from one girl, I recognised no one on the shift and they made no effort to acknowledge me. I found out who I was supposed to be going on after and waited. The clientele was different to Diamonds as we were further into the City; there were more guys in suits but they still held on to a pint and a packet of crisps.

I was the last girl on and my turn soon came round to collect. Within a minute I'd gone round the miserable few customers and was standing impatiently, just waiting for the shift to be over. I went over to the DJ to give him my CD. He was a big, chubby guy called Robert.

'Ain't seen you before, darlin'. You new?'

He was so slimy, holding my hand when I gave him the CD – you know how some men do that? I hated it. He was just a creep but he wasn't nasty or mean. He was actually good-humoured and when I gave him my icy look and a wry smile that said 'don't fuck with me' he laughed and joked, almost as if he knew what he'd done.

'Oh! Chill out luv, just bein' friendly, I'm not that bad you know.'

He was right, he wasn't that bad. But I wanted people to respect my limits. I made it very clear from day one as I always did with people who I suspected wanted to get too physically close that I was not the kind of girl you could paw. I'm not the most tactile of people at the best of times. I'd watched him cuddle and kiss the girls whether they were happy about this or not, so I laid down the law almost immediately. He wasn't all bad though. In fact he was one of the funniest people I'd ever worked with, a real entertainer, always singing and joking and brilliant on the microphone. He was one of those larger-than-life characters. Cocaine can amplify that effect, though, and in this business coke was everywhere.

Once I was on stage the tension melted away. This time I hadn't dosed myself up with alcohol but my nerves appeared to be holding up pretty well. The smaller stage made it easier to command things as did the size of the venue itself: it was about a third the size of Diamonds. I'd also started to realise that dancing to my own choice of music was quite helpful, even liberating. It made it seem much more like you were in control and for me that was very important. The outfit changes and choosing your music made me feel more individual. The shift flew by. I was asked for a few private dances, avoided the manager and by the end of the shift, felt Robert fully understood my position on being too tactile. I didn't have to work hard and made a hundred pounds. Again, this was not big earnings as far as stripping went but I was more than happy with it for such a short and easy shift.

That week I was given two more cancellations; the first was a Wednesday late shift at Pearls. This time I went to great lengths not to be late. It was much busier than I'd previously seen it. There were over twenty guys, all in suits, and the atmosphere was buzzing. This felt much better. I put my name down straight away and saw that I was third: those girls were seriously quick off the mark. Then I went into the changing rooms to get ready. I tended to prepare at home so most of my routine was done there, but I kept the little things to do at work, like touching up my makeup, running straighteners through my hair one more time and the all-important moisturising.

Some of the girls do everything at work. They come in wrapped up in coats and sunglasses looking pretty uninteresting and then they come out two skin shades darker, hair twice as long and appear to be six inches taller. I've seen some amazing transformations, really good ones. Of course it helps if you're naturally attractive and are in good shape to start with. The less you have the more work you have to do to create the illusion. In that respect I was lucky. I knew I had a good body and was regarded as pretty. It made life that little bit easier. And being fair meant I had a hell of a lot less grooming to do in the body hair department.

The changing room at Pearls had enough space to sit and do your makeup without a constant battle for mirror space. I applied my war paint, put on my new black babydoll and headed out to the floor for a quick drink. This was the busiest I'd seen the place and all of a sudden I felt nervous. You didn't want that to happen, not here of all places, because of the stage being lower and not partitioned in any way from the rest of the room. I took a deep breath, told myself it was OK and went and got my jug. I noticed I had the moody little DJ from Diamonds again and scanned the crowd. The fact that I thought this place was a dump didn't stop it being filled with men in suits, some of them very well dressed.

I hadn't even been on stage yet and was asked for a dance, which was a good start. It was ten pounds a dance here and they weren't hard to get. I much preferred private dancing here to being on the stage. It wasn't just that the private dance was one on one; you also didn't have to get close to the guy as you were on a small platform with a pole more than an arm's length away. You didn't have to worry about men trying to touch you as they did at Strings – there it was a nightly hazard of the job. Having a trusty pole to hold on to also meant you didn't have to worry about your balance, especially after a few drinks! You could be more creative and so dancing wasn't as boring. Also this was how you earned the most money: the stage shows were just a shop window advertising the private dances.

One of the things I had to learn here was how to get through the jug collection ritual without making myself late for my stage dance. The problem was that guys always wanted your time – after all, part of the reason they're there is to get some attention from you. Some want more. Some want less. You have to be prepared to brush them off without denting their precious egos – just as you would in the real world. I was reminded of this when I was taking my jug around: I took so long I almost missed my slot on stage.

'Don't stop and talk to them, as you'll never get around everyone and you'll lose money,' one of the girls advised me.

'I know, but they keep stopping me and asking me questions.'

'They always do, but you have to give them the brush-off. Tell them you'll come back, but then don't bother, or say, "I wish I could stop and chat but I have to get round with my jug and I'll get in trouble if I don't." Just be really sickly sweet and flirty – it works every time.'

My next jug was so much quicker as I put the girl's tips into practice. Her name was Dominica; she was a loud and slightly crazy French girl who was great fun and gave me loads of good advice. I may have left Strings an experienced dancer but here I was just a babe in the woods.

That night I did quite a few dances and got a few good tips in my jug – anything over a pound is a tip, but you get the odd five or ten pounds which is always nice. It'd been a good night, I'd made good money and a new friend in Dominica. I went home in a happy frame of mind and felt that things were working out. Little did I know what was to come.

Chapter 13

❧

The jug is half empty

I was booked in for a late Friday shift at Diamonds. Dominica had told me to get there early as there would be a lot of competition to get there first. Even though I arrived an hour before the shift, I was still only number six. I'd never seen it so packed: there were about sixty people in there. Later on I'd discover this was a relatively quiet Friday as they often got over a hundred men. But for now, sixty was daunting enough as I forced my way through the crowd to get to the bar, and then back again to the changing room.

With girls from the current shift and girls turning up for the late shift, the room was absolutely heaving. There was no room to change.

'You don't have to change here, you know.'

It was a girl I hadn't spoken to before.

'Some of us change in the toilets at the back of the club. Come on.'

Her name was Chantal and again I was lucky enough to find someone who took me under their wing. The noisy, boisterous crowd was unsettling me. We had a few drinks before we headed to the toilets to get ready and she gave me her thoughts as to what to expect.

'You have to be really fast with the jug tonight. I mean *really* fast,' she told me.

'Right, so I just do what I've been doing.'

'No, you can't go around one by one. You have to ask them all at once otherwise you'll never get it done before you're up and you'll miss out on money.'

Oh boy.

I was feeling a little worried now but I reasoned that it was better to be informed than not. Chantal was right: it was no picnic. I didn't make it all the way round the crowd with my first jug. Working my first seriously busy night, I found out it wasn't the easy money I first thought it was. I hated that fucking jug. I hated the guys who'd grab your bum as you were going round and try to grab you elsewhere, even attempting to open the clasp of your bra. Some refused to pay, some were rude, some told you to fuck off or said they'd paid already. There were loads of excuses and apparently this was what passed for a mild night.

By the time I was called up to the stage, I'd only got round two-thirds of the crowd and only two-thirds of those had paid. I felt dazed and exhausted: it was so incredibly stressful and now the last thing I wanted to do was get up and dance. I picked the shortest song I had and got my stage show over and done with. I was angry and resentful that I had to be naked in front of people who were so rude and arrogant, plus it was really hot on stage and there was a thick blanket of smoke choking you as you danced. I came off stage and headed for the toilets in a huff, even though there were guys who wanted dances with me.

Thank God Chantal was there to give me more words of wisdom and calm me down.

'Look, every guy has to pay and you have to demand it,' she told me. 'And if they say they've paid, 95 per cent of the time they're talking shit. So *make* him pay and if he refuses threaten him with the bouncers. Most of them won't be willing to risk that.'

'And if that doesn't work, what do I do? These guys are absolute fuckwits, they just ignore me,' I said, sounding really pathetic.

'So call the bouncers and let them deal with it. And just move on.'

Chantal's advice made a difference. When it came time to go around with my next jug I was armed and dangerous and made it nearly all the way through, although I wouldn't say it was hassle-free. More guys paid, that's for sure, and I put up with less shit, but they were still rude and obnoxious. They just want to put you down to make themselves feel better. I knew I had to control my anger but it was getting increasingly difficult. Hellish as it was, I survived the night and did OK out of it. Loads of men wanted dances so it turned out to be a financially rewarding night. Thinking it couldn't get any worse than this, I decided to keep going.

On starting at Diamond and Pearls, I was warned about a stripper called Mina. Nobody said she'd cause me trouble or that she was especially nasty, just that she was the top earner and a real businesswoman, so competition would not be taken kindly. And apparently I was seen as her direct competition.

From the way the other girls spoke I was expecting to meet a goddess. She was a pretty, statuesque Eastern European. She was heavily tanned, in her mid- to late thirties, and as soon as I saw her I knew she was a serious high-maintenance dancer. There was nothing about her that didn't have a designer label. This is where I first saw the Juicy Couture tracksuit (like Jimmy Choo shoes and designer bags, it's a real strippers' favourite). Mina drove a Porsche, had a Louis Vuitton trolley case, expensive bleached hair extensions halfway down her back and a year-round tan hidden under a thick layer of designer makeup. All of her work clothes were La Perla or some other exclusive lingerie brand; she certainly never scrimped. When I first started, she said very little but was clearly aware of me, looking me up and down, watching me work and taking in every little detail. Like her I was a money earner, only younger and fresher.

Usually on the nights she worked she'd be surrounded by her big-spending regulars who kept her occupied. She'd drink champagne with them and work them like the true professional she was: she had the ability to make guys fall in love with her and unashamedly bleed them of all their cash. She attracted the really rich, older guys who responded to her expensive lingerie and immaculate, groomed appearance, but also because she was a seriously classy girl. She was well spoken, incredibly elegant and would only drink the most expensive champagne the bar had. But even when she was sat with her regulars she'd always have one eye on me. When there were no customers to lavish money and gifts on her, she had to work the floor like the rest of us and that presented her with a little problem: I was taking her business. We were directly in competition but I was much younger and softer and the kind of guys you get in pubs seemed to like that.

But Mina was a clever girl. She didn't want to let her earnings slip – she clearly had a very expensive lifestyle to maintain – so instead of trying to get me sacked or being a bitch, she would try to drag me around with her to get the guys to do 'doubles'. This is what I call an intelligent stripper. Mina could have just turned into a jealous bitch and made my life hell, but she used the situation to her advantage not to lose out and if anything, earn even more. 'Doubles' is when two guys take two girls for a dance – some guys prefer this as they would rather go in with a mate than alone. It's good for the girls as one guy will always be up for it and make the other guy go or treat him. If I wasn't busy enough on my own I'd go with her, since it was financially in my interest to do so.

We ended up getting on well. Apparently every year this one customer of hers would fly her best friend – also a pretty blonde – over from somewhere in Eastern Europe and then fly them both to meet him on his yacht where they would sail around the Caribbean or some other exotic location for a few weeks. She and her friend would each come back with a nice wedge of cash and shopping bags filled with clothes, makeup, perfume, jewellery, lingerie – pretty much anything that took their fancy while they were there. The funny thing was that Mina's friend wasn't a dancer or a hooker, just a normal girl with a normal job in an office somewhere who would take this annual holiday. So for three or four weeks of the year she was technically a prostitute, while the rest of the time she just got on with her daily life! I guarantee neither of them would ever class this as prostitution nor even admit to sleeping with the guy. Even with someone I'm dating, I'm the sort of person who doesn't like to be paid for all the time. Maybe I'm overly cautious or a prude.

Mina left within six months of me starting. I have no idea why but I'm positive she wasn't sacked as she was good friends with the boss. Maybe she bagged a rich guy? I wouldn't be surprised and I don't see any other way she would have left the job.

She was one of a number of foreign girls I worked with. Diamonds and Pearls differed from Strings in that respect. Whereas Peter Stringfellow liked to employ English girls, here it was full of foreigners. The boss had a penchant for pert little Brazilian girls but there were also Russians, Poles, Hungarians, Italians and a few American girls. The English girls were actually in the minority. It was really weird at first as the nationalities stayed in their groups and didn't mix, with the exception of the Russian girls, who tended to be really friendly. One of the main reasons for this was the language barrier, but it made things awkward, especially with the Brazilian girls who for some reason were the hardest ones to get on with. There would be multiple conversations in multiple languages going on in the changing rooms and sometimes you'd know that they were talking about you – as the Brazilians did in Portuguese – but there wasn't a thing you could do about it. This was slightly disconcerting but something I would have to get used to.

The only time it was a real problem was when you were working a quiet shift and the other four girls on your shift happened to be unfriendly Brazilians. You'd spend four hours on your own looking at the carpet. But all in all I was happy with things. Due to the shifts being so short I had much more time on my hands, was earning great money without the pressures of a high house fee to cover every night, and was making some really good friends.

A few of the girls I'd known at Strings soon came to Diamonds. It seemed that it was getting harder to make money at Strings, partly because there were now more strip clubs opening up in London and it was becoming big business. The girls were working their butts off to scrape by and they soon saw it didn't have to be like that. Tamara, my closest friend, was the first to come over, followed by Patricia, who left a few months later when she 'found God' and started to work for a gas company. (I'm not joking.) It made me feel good having old friends come over and I'd also made some new ones.

Sometimes going to work was like a night out. You were surrounded by friends, having a laugh and you went home with a few hundred pounds in your pocket. I tried not to mix business with pleasure too much, though.

As I made friends, I also started to hear stories about the two clubs, mostly involving the people who owned them: 'Donnie' and 'Marie'. They were your East London gangster-wannabe types with their hands in all different types of businesses. She was the brains and he was just lucky that Marie involved him in anything. I met Donnie first and he really was one of the dullest, most unintelligent men I have ever come across – and that's saying something given the calibre of guys I've encountered in this business. He had no business sense but a quasi-professional dedication to shagging Brazilian strippers. Being the boss, this wasn't something he had to work hard at and being married with kids didn't appear to get in his way. He hated me and I was later told that he disliked me as I was 'too intelligent' and he couldn't have a conversation with me. This suited me perfectly as I thought he was a dimwit. Donnie liked girls that were all over him and there were plenty of girls who thought that by doing that they'd do even better at work. I was in his bad books and it didn't bother me – at least not until the end of my career there.

Marie, on the other hand, was a hard businesswoman,

the brains of the outfit, the Eastender with the 'heart of gold' – if you managed to find it. As much as I despised her, I had to admire her. She'd built up a fantastic business empire that included the several strip pubs and property. And that was just the stuff I'd heard about. She was a loud, brash, scary character who all the girls feared and many of them were desperate to be in her good books. Marie was both aggressive and humorous; a proud racist who openly said she didn't want any blacks in her club. If a girl gained weight she'd be down on her immediately, telling her in front of everyone, 'You're too fat. No more shifts until you lose some of that weight.' This sort of behaviour wasn't out of the ordinary: I've also heard her tell girls they could only work for her if they had a 'boob job' and the girls would go and do it.

Once she even told me that I'd lost too much weight and on no account was I to lose any more. She ruled with an iron fist. If she didn't like your outfit she'd make the point loudly, making sure that you and everyone else around knew that you looked like shit and had to change straight away. Any flaw – be it cellulite or a bad hair day – that came to her attention would result in the unlucky girl being publicly humiliated. Luckily she'd only come in to check on her empire on Friday nights so we all made sure we had our act perfectly together then. The girls would have freshened up their fake tan, got their nails done that day and be wearing their best outfits. Of course her attitude made sense: you only wanted your girls to be at their very best but the way she communicated it was harsh.

Like Donnie, she had her favourites and if she liked you, you were safe. If not, she could make your life hell. I was one of the fortunate ones. It helped that I fitted her ideal criteria: English, thin, no obvious flaws, hard-working and always well presented. With the exception of the odd comment – because she just couldn't help herself sometimes – she was always courteous and nice to me. When she chose to she could be quite a good person, and you had to admire her brains and sass, but you were always on edge with her as she could turn at any given moment. Marie's opinions on the state of things in the world were pretty rough and uninformed, but she was street smart and in her line of work that counted for more. She also had great breasts, which she'd often whip out at parties.

I was told about the shooting in my first few months of working for Donnie and Marie, and it really shook me up. As well as opening my eyes to a whole other world it made me think about what kind of danger I might be putting myself in. Basically, Donnie pissed a few people off. Apparently he was acting the big man, swaggering a bit too much, and he crossed the wrong people. I don't know exactly what went on but a few days later when he was standing outside the club with the doorman and the doorman's mate, a car drove past and opened fire. The doorman was shot more than once and his friend had multiple wounds. Donnie only got a flesh wound but, being Donnie, he rolled around on the floor like he was about to die.

So the only person who was badly hurt was the innocent bystander who didn't even work there. After that they offered him a job as a doorman which, somewhat oddly, he took. Clearly being shot hadn't put him off! I didn't really know much more about the incident than what people told me; apparently they knew the people who did the drive-by and as often happens with gang wars, they didn't go to prison because it would have been more trouble for all concerned and the police knew that. Over the years I heard a lot about the gangs that run London. I wouldn't dare mention names – my life wouldn't be worth living – but I was slowly made aware of things you think only happen in movies. I've heard stories of kneecapping ordered on one boss of a club and of course rumours of bribes and threats. It was stuff worthy of a movie. But I kept well away from it and was not interested in knowing any more, which I'm sure you can understand.

Chapter 14

Drunk, desperate and deranged

It's funny how, almost subconsciously, you adapt to things. Thinking back to how I felt about the pubs when I first saw them and the early problems I'd had, it all seemed to be in the past now. I was working hard and knew more people than I ever had so was feeling pretty settled. Sure, I didn't think much of the owners, and there were some bitchy girls, but they were an occupational hazard.

There was one in particular called Mariella who was pissed before every shift. Mariella was older and she looked haggard but she kept her job because Donnie was shagging her sister. She'd get drunk and then turn on me, hurling loud insults in my direction or sitting with a customer knocking back shots of tequila and slagging

me off. I was more entertained by her than offended, as
she was in such a bad state. In truth she was embarrassing more than anything else and never dared say a
word directly to me or confront me. I was twice her size
and pretty thick-skinned and would never pull her up on
her drunken behaviour. She didn't bother me too much;
half the time she was barely audible. What really got me
though was when my friend Tamara came to work with
us. Mariella decided to turn her brand of nastiness
against Tamara and would frequently bully her. Tamara
was tiny but if you knew her you'd know that she was
far from a pushover. Nevertheless, because she was a
new girl she didn't want to rock the boat, especially since
it would probably be her who got sacked. She was upset
about it though. I could see that.

One night I saw Tamara go into the toilet closely
followed by Mariella. 'Here she goes again,' I thought. I
decided I'd better follow them and see what was going
on. Mariella and Tamara were arguing; actually it was
more a case of Mariella shouting at Tamara so I stepped
in and broke it up, telling Mariella to basically fuck off
and leave Tamara alone. She slapped me hard on the
thigh and ran out. Tamara and I were in hysterics: it was
something you would expect from an out-of-control
toddler. Of course she went straight to Donnie to make
up some story about how we'd picked on her. Little did

she know there were already lots of complaints about her and there was actually a camera in the toilet to prove she was lying. A few weeks later she got sacked, not solely because of that incident but because she was an embarrassment and I'm guessing Donnie got tired of shagging her sister, Candy, because a few weeks after that she disappeared as well.

Although Candy was an alcoholic, she was actually really sweet. She was an older girl who'd been dancing for well over ten years. I imagined that she was very beautiful in her heyday but the stripping lifestyle hadn't been kind to her. Still, you had to hand it to her, she was pretty good and, even though she was constantly drunk, she had a decent following of eager men. I remember her telling me once she'd been engaged about eight times and had kept all the rings. After she and Mariella were sacked I heard they went to work in a really nasty pub, which was infamous for going beyond the usual limits of strip clubs (the girls allowed the men to touch them, quite intimately in some cases). Like many girls in their mid- to late thirties, they found it impossible to quit and now they were both past their prime, had no choice but to keep going.

One day I arrived to work the middle shift. There were police in the club and a definite buzz that something was happening.

'What's going on?' I asked the barman.

'Some weird guy with a camera, apparently.'

According to witnesses, this guy looked *very* dodgy and seemed to be hiding something under a newspaper. One of the girls on stage saw that he had a video camera. She told the manager who called the bouncers and took the camera away. Naturally the manager looked at the contents of the camera, thinking there might be pictures of the strippers. It was worse. On the tape were pictures of women on escalators – the guy had actually put the camera up their skirt. He'd done it on the tube and in fitting rooms as well as several strip clubs. I'm not sure what action the police took, but it certainly was a salacious bit of gossip in the club for the next few days.

While there have been times where I've felt emotionally fragile while stripping, I've never felt vulnerable in a physical way. Perhaps that's because I'm physically quite strong and also had already survived some pretty horrendous things. One summer's night after a tiring but rewarding shift, I took a cab home to my flat in North London. I did this every night, using the minicab firm next door to the pub. As we were driving, I heard the driver mumbling to himself in another language, but I couldn't tell what it was. He almost seemed to be arguing with himself. I decided then that I didn't want him to drop me in front of my block of flats – I lived in a quiet street with three blocks of newly built flats – so I asked him to stop at the first block at the entrance to the road where I lived. I paid my usual fare, which was always the same, added a £2 tip and quickly got out. That's when the trouble started.

The cab driver got out and stood with his door open, shouting at me. I don't think it had anything to do with the cab fare. He was just nuts. He called me a slut and a whore. I slammed the door and started to run and the next thing I knew he was driving, mounting the kerb and headed for me. I dived into the bushes as the car hit the back of my legs. I landed half in the bushes, half on the pavement. He reversed and drove off.

Within minutes my neighbours were outside helping me. They'd heard me screaming and seen him hit me and drive off. Someone had called the police but I was in shock and just wanted to get into my flat. The next morning my whole body hurt. I had bruising and scraping down one side of my face, and pretty much down one side of my body. My calves were aching and my feet hurt: the car must have just caught the back of my legs in mid-dive and because I was wearing flip flops my feet were pretty battered.

I went straight to the police station to report it and they said it'd been reported the night before and that a patrol car had visited the scene. I returned home after being told I would be visited by an officer at some point: they had taken my details and a very brief account but that was about it. I then called work to cancel as there was no way I'd be working any time soon, the state I was in. I was traumatised. When I called in, everyone already knew. The manager – the gay Aussie guy who was mean to me on my first shift at Pearls – got on the phone asking how I was and explained that, after the incident, the cabbie had gone back to the club, woken the manager in an absolute state of panic and told him what he'd just done. The club had been trying to call me but my phone had stopped working when I hit the ground, so they couldn't get through. I passed the police the information of his admission to my boss and left it with them to investigate. About three or four weeks later I was back at work, and a few months after that the police dropped the case due to insufficient evidence.

What actually happened was that when he was interviewed, the cabbie said I'd kicked his car and he'd responded only by shouting. He said this even though there were witnesses who saw him drive into me. The police told me that he was bringing a case against me for criminal damage and that unless I accepted a caution, they could not pursue my case as there was conflicting evidence. I maintained that I had never kicked his car – I was wearing flip flops, for God's sake – but accepted the caution as I'd promised myself to see this through to the end, as the guy was totally mad and I figured there was so much evidence he would definitely go down for this. How wrong I was!

I ended up being the victim twice over. But that's the system for you. I received a caution and a criminal record for three years and was photographed and fingerprinted after being hit by a madman who drove off and left me on the ground. He got off absolutely scot-free despite the fact that the evidence against him appeared overwhelming: I had significant injuries, there were witnesses and he'd admitted it to my boss. The police got a result that in my eyes was shockingly unfair and wrong. I remember getting the call to say the case had been dropped. I broke down in tears. I was devastated, not only that he had got off but that I'd accepted a caution because the police had told me that was the only way he would be charged. I felt so let down and betrayed by the police, I felt I had been done a huge disservice, and screwed over by the system.

Within a week of this incident I started taking driving lesson as I never wanted to take a taxi alone again. Within a month I'd done my theory, taken an intensive course of lessons and passed my test. I did it on an automatic as I was in such a rush to pass. I immediately bought a second-hand Peugeot and within a week of returning to work, I was driving myself there. Even though driving in London was terrifying in itself, I was happy knowing that I never again had to get in a taxi – and I continued not to use cabs for years afterwards.

Now I was driving and back on track, my main and only concern was earning money, which I was doing pretty easily. With that success inevitably came jealousy. As I've said, there were quite a few bitchy girls among the strippers but because I had my friends I could handle it – or had managed to until now. If you're doing well, this can make girls hate you and want to bring you down. If this job taught me one thing about human nature it's that some people need to hate others; they can't allow themselves to bê happy. Hatred and anger are central to their lives and when you put them in a competitive situation it brings out the worst in them. I think one of the reasons I survived in this poisonous environment – and let's face it, lots of workplaces are the same – is that I didn't concern myself with being the 'best' girl or earning the most money. I set my own targets and didn't compare myself to other girls, whether it was how they looked or what they were earning.

There will always be someone better than you at something and the sooner you accept it, the sooner you can live your life. It's not easy. Imagine if you had to put yourself out there with ten other girls, barely dressed, stood next to you, and people would stand 'viewing' you, looking you up and down, passing judgement solely on how pretty you are or how fat or thin you are or how big your boobs are, how nice your hair is, or your skin or your height and picking the girl next to you time after time – it would naturally start to affect you after a while. This is why there are so many problems between the girls. There is a lot of stuff going on, above and below the surface.

I've been lucky in that I've never really had to hustle. I often just stood on a spot at the back of the room and guys would approach me for a dance. I stood there doing nothing, or so they thought. I was actually working the room the whole time but doing it in a very subtle way. My eyes would catch a customer's eye, hold his gaze and look away bashfully. Then he'd come and ask me for a dance. This was just my own method of working and it really did work for me, to the annoyance of the other girls.

It pissed off some of the girls since they had to go around asking guy after guy for dances, which isn't much fun as you can feel like you're begging. There was a girl called Jane who detested me: she was a pretty girl, but slightly chubby and not particularly striking in any way. We spoke to each other and got on OK but it was uneasy. I knew she was a very jealous person, not just of me but of anyone as she would always be bitching about someone. But her attitude got her into trouble when she went to join a modelling agency.

At her interview with the agency she noticed a picture on the wall of a recent magazine spread I'd done. Jane thought it would be clever to tell the agent to be wary of me as apparently I was also a well-known prostitute. Little did she know that the girl she was speaking to was one of my friends, a girl I'd known for over three years. Within minutes of Jane leaving the office, I'd been told and I was steaming. There was no way I was letting that one go. I told a few of my friends what had happened and Jane soon found out, was calling me a liar, telling people I was jealous of her and all the usual crap. So I just stopped talking to her. But it didn't end here: she instigated a hate campaign against me, badmouthing me to just about every girl at the club. She'd tell them I was a hooker, I'd stolen from her and that I wasn't to be trusted. She'd tell anyone who'd listen how she knew people where I'd worked before and she'd been warned about me.

It wouldn't have really affected me but people believed her and actually stopped talking to me. I wasn't prepared to go around defending myself against her slander; my close friends knew the truth and that's what mattered. I was upset, though. Every time a new girl would start, she would do the 'friendly thing' and warn them about me.

I didn't know any of this for a long time. It was only when a girl who I'm now friends with told me, that I realised Jane had been orchestrating this campaign against me where she'd tell new girls that speaking to me meant that nobody else would speak to them. I did lose friends as a result and was really unhappy at work. She also did little things to annoy me, like copying outfits I bought. But I knew I had to keep focused on my work as the only way I could get under her skin was to earn more and more and be that much better than her so she knew I was in a different league.

Underneath it was getting to me and I felt myself becoming much harder as a way of dealing with it. If I didn't toughen up I wouldn't be able to work as I'd be crying. I really concentrated on my work, would hardly speak to anyone and just became really tough. If none of my friends were working on my shift, I'd get changed, work and barely say a word to anyone. I also made sure I always looked as perfect as I could on every shift, just to piss her off. People thought this change in me was because I thought I was so much better than everyone else and saw me as arrogant. I didn't care about them. I was earning more money than pretty much anyone else and that was the point of all this. I never, ever forgot that.

Meanwhile my landlord decided that he wanted to sell his flat – and so I faced upheaval again. My goal had always been stability and a place that would be a haven for me, so I made the life-changing decision to buy a flat. I'd had an accountant since my Strings days to help me with my tax, but now I was intent on saving as much of my money as I could. From the moment I realised I wanted a flat I rarely went out and almost never bought clothes or shoes. I'd always been a saver rather than a spender but now I had a goal and it made even more sense to me. Work suddenly became a lot easier and I actually worked even harder and pushed myself to earn more. So while I was getting happier, more affluent and accomplished, I was also getting more envied, hated and ostracised. But everything comes at a cost and for now it was a price I was prepared to pay.

I was being obsessively careful with my money. If I earned three hundred and eight pounds in a shift, I saved three hundred and lived off eight pounds until my next shift. All I cared about was saving the rest of the money I needed for my deposit. I had a few months before having to leave the flat so I worked as many shifts as I could, did every cancellation shift they had available and lived off nothing. I picked the area I wanted to live in – close to work, but not too close – and started the very exciting and slightly frustrating process of flat hunting.

At first I hated everything I was shown. I was moving from a relatively poor area to Docklands, which was anything but poor. So my expectations were a little flattened. I soon realised that to get anything even half as good as I expected I had to increase my budget. I decided to keep on looking until I found the perfect flat. And I did. For me, anyway. It was pretty trashed and had purple walls and pink carpets but I knew I could make it work. And so I became the owner of my first flat. It was the most incredible feeling to have a place of my own, a place I'd worked for! I felt protected but also a little scared because I'd taken on a mortgage which seemed very large. Still, it was fine as long as I was earning the sort of money I was earning now. If anything went wrong, I could always take on a lodger or rent it out and move somewhere cheaper.

I remember bringing my mum and David, her partner, to the flat for the first time. They arrived laden with paint cans and tools and were so excited for me. With their help I painted the walls, laid a wooden floor, changed the doors and made it into a home. I still had a lot to do, but luckily I had all of my furniture, so I was happy and everything else could wait. I carried on working hard, slowly doing things in my flat bit by bit. It was exciting but tiring because I was still doing the extra shifts.

Chapter 15

❧

Up close and personal

Without realising it my life had gone back to how it was at Strings – all work and no play. Even though I'd finished renovating my flat, the constant work and lack of social life continued as I found myself once again consumed by the stripping world. Keeping busy meant I didn't have to think about how empty, lonely and superficial my life actually was, but it was a vicious circle: if I didn't slow down I'd never have a crack at a so-called 'normal' life and a relationship.

Some people might call my reluctance to get involved with men 'commitment issues' but personally I don't believe there is such a thing: it's about meeting the right person – or about being sensible about what works. I've never been one for serial dating and find the whole process very off-putting. The thought of sitting through dinner with a total stranger trying to make polite

conversation is not appealing to me and neither are one-
night stands: I've never had one in my life and never
wish to. Maybe I just don't want to give myself away
too easily, maybe it's a reaction to what I've seen stripping or maybe I figured out early on how pointless they
are – for me, anyway.

I know I'm wary of men getting too emotionally close
to me. I'm not one to put my heart on the table and I'm
not very tactile. It takes me a while before I'll display my
affection and tell a guy how I feel about him. Guys have
said I have a steel wall around me. I remember Andy, a
guy I went out with for over a year – I saw him once a
week and rarely allowed him to stay with me –
constantly telling me I needed to be more affectionate.
Months later, for Christmas, he bought me a great T-
shirt which said, 'My boyfriend said I needed to be more
affectionate so I got two' – boyfriends, that is.

That about summed up every relationship I ever had.
I would date someone for a year or two, never let them
get close and restrict my affections. They would fall in
love with me and I would love them, but if I was honest
with myself I only loved them as friends. I believe that
if you spend long enough with someone it's only
natural that you will love them; you just need to be
sensible enough to separate friendship, need and
companionship from real love. Whenever there was any

mention of anything serious I would run. They loved me and I could never return that love, let alone give anything more.

While I was working I had little or no interest in sex. I'm not going to psychoanalyse myself too much, but I think you give away so much of your sexuality when you're stripping that your sex drive almost completely disappears – it did with me anyway. I'm sure those who take an academic viewpoint on these things might say it's because I hated men and couldn't see them as potential partners. I've read that somewhere. I think 'hate' might be too strong a word, but if you're stripping night after night you learn to turn off your normal emotions: you don't see the men you're dancing for as men that you would relate to in a social context and therefore you don't feel horny about them, no matter how attractive they are. I'd also made a conscious decision at the start that I would never mix business with pleasure and so for me they were just sources of income.

At the same time I was playing a role. My life as a dancer revolved around being this sexy, hot minx; a horny glamourpuss that men desired and worshipped but couldn't have. My persona was being a woman who is totally confident, in control and who probably has several men on the run. In truth, if you met me I'd be the complete opposite of what you'd expect a stripper to be, both in looks and demeanour. I'm not showy, I don't walk into a room and own it and I don't project myself.

When I was dancing my whole existence revolved around being sexy so I guess subconsciously I didn't want that when I was away from work. I was also more interested in earning money than collecting men. I think a lot of strippers go one way or the other: it either empowers them and boosts their sex drive or, like me, saps every bit of sexiness from you so you have a non-existent sex life. It wasn't just that I had to be this amazing, sexy goddess all the time at work, but also that I didn't want to be seen as just that. I wanted to be identified for more and for me that meant seeing myself as more than just a stripper. I was fed up with being something to look at. I wanted to be loved and appreciated, seen as intelligent, thoughtful or funny – anything but a piece of meat, a dumb blonde that was no more than a body.

My instinct, when I wasn't at work, was to cover up and try to appear as non-sexual as possible. I was very prudish, always covered from head to toe in the most unrevealing outfit, never wearing heels. I lived in loose jeans and tracksuits. Dressed like that I would curl up on my sofa and read. I'd always been pretty well informed about current affairs but I found that being in a business where my body was the focus made me want

to be more learned. I developed a love of English literature and anatomy and my brain started whirring with
possibilities, such as courses and university. These never
materialised, but when I wasn't working I would spend
my time teaching myself, constantly reading about
architecture, art, history and medicine. So instead of
being a normal girl in her early twenties with a healthy
and active love life, I was becoming the exact opposite
of my 'character'.

Still I tried to do my best to get on with people at
work. I've mentioned one of the DJs, Terry, the strange,
moody little guy who said very little and had an almost
permanent scowl on his face. Terry was best friends
with Marie, the owner of both Diamonds and Pearls.
Apparently he'd known her for years. He'd go to her
house for dinner all the time, so naturally he thought he
had a privileged position. He didn't talk to me much
but then he suddenly started being nice to me. We got
on well and I thought, 'This guy's not such an arsehole,
actually.'

A few weeks after we started chatting he asked me to
go to his annual golfing ball with him. I flatly refused. I
wasn't mean or disrespectful in any way; I didn't want
to go with him and I'm not someone who beats
about the bush. After this episode we barely spoke for
months and I was told I'd probably committed

professional-stripping suicide because he was one of the head honchos. Other girls told me I should keep him sweet or he'd make my life pure hell. I was also told he'd had a few girls sacked in the past and the most astonishing thing of all, he had 'dated' – and I use that term very loosely – many a stripper and always took a pretty blonde to his yearly golf party. So for a man who, bizarrely, was used to girls falling at his feet or at least kissing his butt, I was bad news. He was also a short, fat, middle-aged man – so how he got these luscious women was beyond me. But then there was a great deal about this business that I found strange.

After my blunt refusal to go out with him, he decided to be a bastard to me, giving me short jugs on a busy night. Let me explain: you'd usually have ten minutes to collect from everyone. He would give me six minutes so I'd earn less money and get seriously stressed. Then he'd bark at me to get on stage, saying I was late. Not only would that embarrass me in front of the customers but it would get me into trouble with the managers, and he knew it! He'd also leave me up on stage for an inordinate amount of time – each song should be four minutes long but he'd have me up there for six or seven, which was hell: trying to do the same limited dance moves in front of a drunken unappreciative audience is bad enough for four minutes, let alone any more.

This went on for a month or two and as was my way, I tried not to let it get to me. I didn't work every shift with him, just two or three per week and 90 per cent of the time I ignored him. But one day he was so utterly rude to me. He shouted and swore at me in front of the customers. I can't remember what set him off; maybe he was just being a bastard for the sake of it. In any case, enough was enough. I screamed and swore back at him and from that day on we got along brilliantly – for the time being anyway. When I got my flat in Docklands, he lived nearby so he asked for lifts home when we worked together. I didn't mind. He knew where I stood and it made for a strange alliance. His company wasn't too painful for the ten-minute journey and being in his good books was a hell of a lot better than not. I also got to hear all of the gossip from him; he'd be drunk or stoned and would happily tell me things, including the sordid details of his relationship with a Russian stripper called Natalia.

She was a quiet, sweet, pretty girl who was as timid as a mouse and married to a Russian guy who beat her. She was always bruised, as they would have blazing, sometimes violent, rows due to him being very jealous. Stripping was probably the worst possible career option for her but then again he refused to get a job and would happily spend her money. He would sit at home buying stuff from catalogues, like running machines, clothes and tasteless jewellery, pretty much anything. She should have left him. The problem was that he had an English passport and as his wife, she would eventually get residency after a certain amount of time in the UK. That time was nearly up. It was only a matter of months before she could get her permanent residency, and until then she was stuck. Meanwhile she'd begun an affair with Terry. She would lie and tell her husband she was working or going out with the girls and soon Terry was more than a little infatuated with her. Their affair went on for months; he would constantly buy her presents, beg her to leave her husband and change his shifts so he could work with her.

Knowing she was soon going to leave her husband, she started working very, very hard. At the end of each shift she asked the manager to put half of her earnings in the safe at the club. Knowing that her husband was closely monitoring her money and happily spending it, she was slowly building up a large amount of savings behind her husband's back; soon she was only taking home a third of her earnings – and believe me, she was earning. Her husband would get mad and big arguments would break out as he didn't trust her and would call her lazy or think she was spending money elsewhere. Despite this, she carried on working her butt off and hoarding money.

Having her money in the club safe and knowing it was OK because she was shagging Terry gave Natalia confidence. In the months leading up to her visa application, she appeared a lot braver. This was also helped by all the money she was earning and suddenly she didn't look like a battered woman any more. Instead she looked all-powerful and confident. And because her husband decided she was earning far too little – which she put down to bad shifts, time of year etc. – he agreed to take a job painting and decorating which she found for him. This worked well for her in every sense: the fact that he actually took a job showed she was regaining power and with him working she could hoard more money away. Meanwhile, when he was working in the daytime, she could shag Terry.

And so you won't be surprised to hear that Natalia's husband began to improve. I'm sure it was due to the sudden realisation that he now had less of a hold on her and she might be slipping away from him. Whatever his reasons, there were fewer arguments and he began to treat her well, cooking dinner once in a while and running her a bath after work on occasions. Now she was back and forth between him and Terry. I don't think she ever planned to play them like this; she truly was confused and had feelings for both of them. Even though her visa was imminent she would be in love with her husband one week and in love with Terry the next. This blowing hot and cold meant Terry had no idea where he was and his moods would fluctuate. Everyone knew what was going on – it's hard to keep secrets in a club – as they were always snatching a drink together and he'd find any excuse to sneak down to the changing room.

While Terry was getting messed up, Natalia was shifting between guys and saving up a truckload of cash. I would hear all of the details on our journey home from work. Once, on our way home he was in a foul mood and he threw a plastic bag at me, saying, 'Have this, she doesn't fucking deserve it.'

It was a bag with loads of lip glosses and perfume. I gave it back to him, telling him not to be stupid and things would be good again in a few days.

'Go on, take it. You're always driving me home.'

Since he was threatening to throw it out the window I accepted it – a girl never turns away a free lip gloss! It appeared that Natalia was becoming increasingly bold. I discovered she was lying to her husband, saying she was working when she was actually shagging Terry, who would give her money so her husband would think she'd been working. This smart and highly manipulative girl had not only got her husband to get off his lazy butt and work but she had Terry twirled around her little finger and a lump sum in the safe that must've been at least £15K. When her visa came through, she didn't leave her husband or Terry. She just carried on with her beneficial situation until one day she just disappeared from work. Later Terry told me she just finished with him and he never heard from her again. She'd changed her number and not a soul knew where she was.

It wasn't until months later we found out she had been seeing a customer while also seeing Terry and her husband. (I don't know how she found the time because as well as a husband and two lovers she had seven or eight shifts a week and really worked her butt off!) The customer was married at the time. Eventually, they both divorced their partners, she left work, they bought a house, and as far as I am aware were soon married. Talk about having your cake and eating it!

Chapter 16

∽

Another friend hits the revolving door

Not all the girls who worked at Diamonds and Pearls were fire-breathing dragons – it's just that those ones ruin it for you so they stand out. There were actually some really sweet girls and if you were lucky enough to work the same shift with them it made the evening a whole lot better. There was a slightly older crew who'd seen it all before. They were mainly English, pretty grounded and stayed out of the bickering and politics. One of the girls, who was known on the stripping circuit as Shannon the Cannon, was also one of the sexiest dancers I've seen to date, and would always find a way to defuse an uncomfortable situation by saying something highly inappropriate and easing the tension. She later went on to become a psychotherapist (a favourite course of study with strippers). I often wonder what her clients would think if they knew about her previous career.

There were other girls I could talk to. I was still good friends with Angie, who'd encouraged me to work there in the first place. She was often away, gallivanting in some far-off exotic country on a holiday so I wouldn't see her too much. There were also the girls I met early on, like Dominica and Chantal. About this time a new girl started. Her name was Melissa and from day one, we clicked. Like me, she saw stripping purely as a business, a way of making good money, and had no interest in bagging a rich man or shagging customers. She was, as far as stripping went, a normal girl who came to work, did her job and kept her life separate. To this day, she's the girl I respect the most as she's the only girl I know who's managed to leave the job far behind, use her money relatively wisely, and lead a very happy, stable life. I'm sure that doesn't sound out of the ordinary to you. In fact it may sound dull. But believe me, a girl who gets a husband, house, two kids, a family business and as much happiness as life will allow is a rarity in this business. (Probably a rarity in life, if you think about it.)

Within weeks of Melissa starting work, we struck up an alliance. Unfortunately my joy at meeting her was overshadowed by what happened to Tamara. One night at Pearls, a fight kicked off between Tamara and Terry the DJ. I was working at Diamonds and apparently they had a pretty packed club and Tamara had just finished her jug collection and given Terry her CD. She was ready to go on stage and the guys were lined up waiting for her to dance. Tamara and Terry had never really seen eye to eye, but this night things were about to get worse.

Normally as you go up to the stage he'd announce you with something along the lines of, 'Next up, we have Ellouise.' This is your least friendly announcement.

'Next up, the beautiful Ellouise.' He thinks you're all right.

'You're in for a treat next, guys, because it's the lovely/beautiful/elegant Ellouise.' In other words, he's particularly keen on you.

Now this particular night, Terry had drunk a great deal and probably been smoking weed as well. He was smarting about the business with Natalia and, as Tamara was about to go on stage, all of that and his dislike of Tamara came together in one explosive outburst.

'Next up we have Tamara. Not that you'll want to bother watching her.'

Tamara stood frozen and shocked, thinking she must be dreaming. That didn't just happen to her, did it? It wasn't until a customer said, 'What the fuck's going on? Is he talking about you?' that she realised she wasn't dreaming.

Tamara was too shocked to reply.

Then a young regular stepped in and asked, 'Do you want me to bash him?'

Tamara refused the offer. Meanwhile she now had to take off her clothes in front of fifty or so guys while trying to be sexy. She did her best to hold back her rage and be as professional as possible when really she just wanted to run away and hide – or hit him!

Halfway through her dance, he cut the song, made another nasty comment and she just stood there semi-naked, embarrassed as hell. She then grabbed her clothes and ran off stage.

Angry on her behalf, the customers tried to stop her, saying he was well out of order. Several of them offered to take him outside and give him a 'going over' but Tamara just ran for the changing room. When she got there, the other girls asked what had happened to make him like that. Before she could say anything, Terry burst through the door and headed for Tamara. He grabbed her by the throat and started yelling.

'You ugly fucking black cunt! I hate you, you black cunt! I'll have you shot.'

Terry shared Marie's racist views. The girls in the

changing room were horrified, screaming at him to stop. Jug still in hand, Tamara raised it over her head to hit him. Immediately a girl called Honey stopped her, shouting, 'Don't do it! We've all seen him. He's fucked himself now.'

By this point the manager and a bouncer had run in, the fight was broken up and Terry was taken outside.

Full of tears and rage, Tamara quickly put on her 'outdoor' clothes, ran out and jumped into a cab to go home. Her shift wasn't over but there was no way she was staying.

Meanwhile I was finishing my shift at Diamonds and getting ready to go home. I never hang around. It wasn't until I was on the way home that I realised my mobile was ringing. I waited until the next red light, dug the phone out of the bottom of my bag and saw around forty missed calls. I was five minutes from home, so I waited until I was parked outside my house and picked up the first call that came through.

It was Terry. He was pissed and saying something about Tamara; that she was a troublemaker and the 'black bitch' was trying to make him look bad. I didn't know what to say. He just kept drunkenly mumbling at me while I could see I had a call waiting. I hung up after telling him I'd call him back, and picked up the next call. It was Tamara, who said she'd been trying to call me for hours – just as Terry had. Again my phone was constantly beeping so I cut her off, promising to call her back. I went into the flat and listened to my messages. There were loads from both Terry and Tamara, but also messages from Honey and a few other girls saying that Terry had attacked Tamara in the changing room, she wasn't answering her phone and could I call them.

Wow, this was surreal. Terry was still trying to call – for me a sign of his guilt – so I answered him on about the fifth call, biting my tongue until I heard what he had to say. I didn't get much sense out of him. He was really off his head and was just being abusive and racist, saying he hated Tamara and that she did his head in. I then spoke to Honey, who told me the whole changing room saga. Finally I spoke to Tamara, who told me her side, even though there was only one side to tell, since Terry couldn't do anything but mutter abuse about Tamara.

It was rare to see Tamara buckle under pressure but during the long conversation I had with her she broke down crying. She told me that the words were much more painful that him grabbing her and you could sense both her anger and sadness. We chatted for ages until she was semi-calm and then called it a night. As soon as I got off the phone it carried on ringing. I switched it off. By now my head was spinning and I was exhausted. I went straight to sleep.

A few days later, Tamara was called into the office to speak to Marie. The conversation apparently went from, 'Let me reimburse you for the money you lost that night' and 'Please don't go to the police' to 'Will a few hundred quid help?'

Basically Marie was trying to buy her off without admitting any wrongdoing on Terry's part. Tamara declined, knowing that Marie and Terry were best buddies. Instead she said, 'Suspend him for two weeks, unpaid, or I'll go to the police.'

'You can't go to the police 'cause he'll get banged up. He's not long been done for kicking down his ex's door.'

'Suspend him for two weeks unpaid, that's all I want.'

Of course you're thinking why on earth didn't Tamara go to the police or demand him sacked. Well, you're kind of limited in this job. *You* don't want to get sacked and you know *he* will never get sacked, so you have to negotiate what you can. Marie agreed to her request and he was suspended for two weeks. During those two weeks, he came in nearly every day for a drink and we heard on the grapevine that he was paid the whole time.

Over the next four to five weeks, Tamara tried to get on with her job. She and Terry were put together on as few shifts as possible. Unfortunately that meant that

Tamara missed out on many of the more lucrative late shifts because he was working them. He would still come into work on her shifts even though it was evident he'd been spoken to. He was relatively subdued with pretty much everyone and it was clear he'd been told to keep his head down. But just seeing him and knowing he was around screwed Tamara's head up. Not only was she disgruntled, but it pained her mentally and emotionally to be around, let alone work with, this guy who had physically and racially abused her.

The final straw came when she had an argument with Natalia, Terry's Russian lover. It wasn't even an argument really, just words. I know this because I was there. They were in the toilets and Natalia decided to put her two pence worth in about the whole situation, sticking up for Terry. Natalia insinuated that Tamara was lying and tried to plead Terry's case, saying he was a good man. The toilets emptied very quickly. I know Tamara and when she gets angry it's best to leave her to it. I waited outside the toilet door knowing Tamara could fully handle herself but wanting to be close – just in case. Surprisingly, there was no shouting and screaming. They were just bickering, with Tamara telling her what actually happened on the night in question. It ended with harsh words and Natalia storming out, but nothing more.

Twenty minutes later, at the end of the shift, Tamara

was called out of the changing room. Donnie was working that night (one of his current shags must have been dancing) and called her for a word. She got changed, packed her stuff and ran up to see what the fuss was this time. Apparently, Natalia had complained of a fight in the toilet. Donnie checked the camera and there was Tamara 'strangling' Natalia, just as Terry had done to her. As luck would have it there was visual but no sound in the toilet, so you didn't hear Tamara going through the events of the night and mimicking for Natalia exactly what Terry had done. All you saw was Tamara's action coupled with Natalia's story of the 'fight' in the toilet; you can the guess the rest. Tamara was not even asked her side, just accused of harassing Natalia. This was the final straw for her.

I remember coming up from the changing rooms – they had long since been moved from the cramped dirty little room by the stage to a new, larger space in the cellar – to hear Tamara shouting at Donnie, 'You can stick the lot of you and your fucking job up your arse. Fuck this shit.' And she left. Well, not quite. The door had been locked so there was a slightly comical moment of her shaking a locked door unable to leave with an overweight doorman uncomfortably running to unlock it for her before her dramatic exit. (Tamara and I laugh about this now whenever we tell the story.)

Once I realised what had happened, I ran after her and we sat in my car while she told me the full story. Looking back, there's a very high chance that it was all a set-up to get rid of her. Terry was a racist pig and hated the fact that he had a dressing down from the boss and a two-week suspension when he thought he was untouchable. I think he decided to get her sacked. But that's just my opinion. Either that or it's a hell of a coincidence. Needless to say, I no longer gave Terry a lift home.

Chapter 17

❧

Where's Wally? He's stalking me

Losing Tamara from work was depressing and I felt pretty low. Terry knew she and I were close friends so things were now awkward with him. He and I were civil but kept our distance. I think he realised how much information he'd given me on our journeys home over the previous few months so he knew that it wasn't worth making my life difficult.

There seemed to be quite a few issues brewing among the girls. I wasn't the only one having problems. Angie had left her long-term boyfriend for the doorman – the one who'd been the innocent bystander during the drive-by. It was all a bit of a shock as she hadn't told her friends anything. Everyone thought that she and her partner were happy and settled, but one day it was over and not long after she was seeing Ian, the doorman – and resident drug dealer. He was a muscled meathead covered in tattoos, with bleached blond hair. Not that there's anything wrong with that but Angie was a pretty girl from a fairly middle-class family and it was slightly unexpected. Let's just say he wasn't the sharpest of knives. But it turned out they were very much in love. It didn't stop us all from worrying about her: let's face it, if your mate started dating a bouncer who was known for drug dealing you'd be worried too. Chantal was also in a dreadful situation with a man, except she just didn't see it yet. She was dating an utterly useless guy who walked all over her but, like so many girls, she couldn't see the flaws.

I know it might sound cruel but over the years I found that in order to keep my own life together, I simply couldn't take on anyone else's problems – unless it was one of my best mates. In this industry every girl is constantly having one drama or another so you have to really keep yourself to yourself or you're always involved in something you shouldn't be. It didn't matter: I was about to have my own hassles. There was a guy who'd come in a few times a week and he'd taken a shine to me. He never really had any dances, but would always come in on very dead shifts and give me a tip in my jug so that I would come back and speak to him. He was a lanky pale guy who looked like the character from that kids' book, *Where's Wally?* So that's what I privately called him: Wally. He was very clean-cut and worked in IT for the police. All in all I'd say we'd had about five chats that lasted a few minutes each. Then, one night, I found a bunch of flowers on my car outside work.

This bothered me, since I didn't park directly outside work. You couldn't. That meant that someone had watched me walk to my car. The first time I thought nothing of it, but by the third time it was a bit worrying. Then one day Wally said to me, 'Did you like your flowers?' God – it was only him. I was so relieved because I thought he was pretty harmless and decided that it was just a coincidence that he knew my car. I thanked him but told him he'd scared me, joking that I thought I had a stalker. Over the next few weeks, a barrage of flowers, cards and letters appeared, always on my car windscreen. It was uncomfortable more than anything. When I saw Wally I'd say, 'Thanks but really, you don't have to.' The letters were slightly disconcerting – love letters with poor imitations of poetry. At the time I thought it was nothing I couldn't handle since I'd always accepted unwanted attention as part of the job.

One night as I was driving home from a shift I noticed a car following me. At first I thought I was going mad and seeing things but then I realised it was actually happening. I knew my route well and knew every variation to avoid traffic so I started driving like a maniac, speeding down side roads and pulling manoeuvres that would make James Bond proud. I lost the car and warily made my way home, staying off the main roads and taking the least obvious route possible. It was scary stuff. Knowing I was now safe, I went inside and did my best to forget it but I felt on edge. I was sure it was Wally.

I didn't see him for a few days, until a few nights later when I spotted the same old VW Golf following me. I'm positive he hadn't followed me from the club as the roads were pretty empty and I would have spotted him. He must have picked me up near where he lost me last time. I wasn't far from home so it was harder to lose him. I decided to keep driving past where I lived and phoned a guy I knew, a friend of mine who would do anything for me. He was someone I'd started dating but it had kind of fizzled out: his schedule was just as demanding as mine! We still spoke but we'd happily left it at sending each other the odd text or catch-up phone call. As soon as he heard me on the phone he told me to drive to his house and he and his brother would wait outside for the guy. He lived about fifteen minutes from me so I didn't have far to go. I allowed the car to follow me, called him as instructed when I was a minute away and by the time I'd pulled into his road, he, his brother and some of his friends were running towards my car. When Wally saw me he realised he'd been rumbled and sped off. I was relieved and thought that would be the last of him. I chilled out there for a few hours (still slightly scared in case he was waiting round the corner) and when I was too shattered to wait any longer I drove home.

The next day I had a lunch shift and, believe it or not, Wally came in. He was absolutely furious. He stormed up to me and called me a liar (I had told him I lived in North London, since you never tell punters the truth), saying he thought we were friends and lots of other bullshit besides. Then he left. It threw me a bit but, hoping that was the end of it, I carried on with my shift. Once again, on returning to my car, I had a note. It wasn't nice or romantic this time. He was basically calling me a liar – and making some mildly threatening comments. He did this a few times and, after about the fourth note, I told him I'd alerted the police and the club and that he should stop or I'd take it further. At this point I hadn't told anyone about the notes. I heard nothing for a few more days and decided I'd tell the club, who immediately barred him. The day he tried to get in and realised he was barred, I found this note on the windscreen of my car:

'I hate you, you liar. I hope you and your family die in a thunderstorm.'

I will never forget those final words. How random! It was such a ridiculous threat I couldn't take it seriously. Sure it was scary, but this guy was two sandwiches short of a picnic. I kept my wits about me and was always very alert driving home. It just goes to show that what innocently starts as a meaningless conversation can turn into something much scarier.

The episode had had a greater effect on me than I imagined at the time. I started to become a lot less friendly with customers, and generally less approachable all around. I was already unpopular with the girls but now I was becoming a hard bitch with the customers too. I knew my personality was really starting to change: for a start, I was developing a temper. I became irritable and always seemed to be on edge about something.

A few months after this, my car got keyed. I'd had a big row with Jane a few days earlier, so I had my suspicions. It started when a group of guys wanted six girls to dance for the six of them. There were eight girls on the shift; one was on stage while one was doing her jug, so I ran around rounding the girls up, including Jane, so I could make it happen. She refused. 'I'm not dancing if you're dancing.'

She said this in front of the six customers and all of

the girls. I was really pissed off as I'd run around trying to organise it. The guys were big spenders and regulars of mine and naturally I didn't want to look bad or miss out on money.

'Come on Jane, don't be so pathetic: it's not about me, it's about them; just do the bloody dance.'

'Fuck off.'

'Jane, it's your job, for fuck's sake!'

The guys were getting really annoyed and they were all ready to go into the backroom for their dance. At the same time, the other girls were getting pissed off. I had no choice but to bring the manager over.

'Get in there, Jane, and stop fucking about.'

She sulked but we finally got the dance over and done with, me feeling like an idiot in front of my regulars. The other girls were angry for getting dragged into a situation and she wasn't too happy for getting a rollicking for being a pain in the arse. So when my car got keyed, I had a pretty good idea who it was.

We continued like this over a few weeks, constantly bickering. She'd aggravate me and I'd bite back. We'd be working together and I'd go and change into an outfit only to find out she'd copied me. She started to choose the same music as me and would dance to pretty much every song I danced to. It was like something out of the film *Single White Female*.

I remember when I was putting on a new outfit I'd bought a few weeks before, so it was still lovely and fresh. It feels really nice when you have a new costume. Lo and behold, who comes on to the floor ten minutes later in an almost identical costume she'd nipped out and bought that day.

'For fuck's sake Jane, just grow up,' I said.

It got to the point where I couldn't help myself. It was like having an annoying eight-year-old sister constantly copying you, except this one had a nasty streak. Not long after this I found one of the wing mirrors on my car had been smashed. I hoped it was an accident but when I took it to the shop they told me it'd been smashed downwards, which wasn't accidental. This was frustrating because I could never prove it was Jane. Even so I said nothing as there was no proof and I didn't want her to do something worse.

I did my best to ignore her and to make myself feel better by knowing I was earning more than her. At this point in my life I should have been really happy. I had a beautiful flat of my own, was more financially secure than I'd ever imagined being and was earning a fortune. But if I really stopped and thought about it, I was unhappy. The thing is, when you're dancing, you don't realise how deep you've sunk until it's too late. You get into a rut – one that's filled with money, hate, jealousy and just about every negative emotion you can think of. Yet while you're in this environment, you can't see what's happening to you: instead you keep changing to cope with it. You constantly remind yourself of the good things; the money and the independence it gives you: and that plus the idea of having to find soemthing else to do is enough to keep you there. But at some point there has to be a limit. It's just a case of when you choose to acknowledge it – if you ever do.

Chapter 18

∽

These charming men

How many arguments can you have over a pound? Loads. As I've described earlier, I was never good at my jug. The whole collection thing had never appealed to me and maybe I was quietly rebelling. I was fine when it was quiet but when there are a hundred guys and you're trying to get round all of them it's hard, really hard. To add to the stress of walking through a crowd asking for money, the men can be complete bastards. And I was tired of letting them treat me like shit. I'd never let them walk over me but now my patience was wearing thin.

Language differences mean some girls don't fully understand what the guys say, while others just allow them to get away with it. Sometimes I'd see a guy slap a girl on the bum or pinch her and she wouldn't react. If a guy did it to me I'd go absolutely spare. Depending on what he did and where he touched me I would react appropriately. If a guy tried to brush my bum on a packed night I might give him a dirty look; if he tried to slap my bum or grope me I'd have to react more strongly, maybe a sneaky stiletto heel in the foot or just a rollicking.

There were times when a guy would grab you somewhere else. Make no mistake: this wasn't an accident. They would put their hands between your legs and touch you. As a stripper you tend to develop quick reflexes and pull away fast. That's irrelevant because as far as I'm concerned they've still touched me and it's horrible. You scream, you stamp on his foot, you hit him, you call the bouncer – because in truth you've been sexually assaulted. I don't care what anyone says: it's not part of our job description.

Nothing can prepare you for it and no matter how long you strip, you never ever get used to it. What makes it worse is when the useless doorman (most of them are) doesn't throw him out, so when you're on stage, biting your lip trying not to cry, you see the bastard's face in the audience, smiling up at you. The fact that the club won't even protect you makes it a hundred times worse. If that happened to a girl in any other situation the police would be called on the grounds that she'd suffered a sexual assault. If it happened to you in an office – well, the bloke would be in major trouble. But in a strip club there's not much you can do except protect yourself.

Thankfully this kind of thing didn't happen often; it's the verbal abuse that is far more prevalent. Mostly it only happens on the night shifts since the guys are drunk. When it's busy they think they can get away with anything. You'd get these guys, usually the suits or East London wide boys, who would talk to you like you were shit on their shoe. They seemed to think it was perfectly all right to tell you to fuck off when you asked for a pound. It was not uncommon when taking your jug around to hear things like:

'I'm not paying you, you ugly cunt. You're not worth a pound.'

'I'd rather shut my eyes than see you.'

'Fuck off, you horrible bitch.'

'Go and get a proper job, you dirty whore.'

'One pound in the jug, that must make you a tenner for a fuck (ha ha ha).'

Now I couldn't ignore this and there was no reason why I had to. Yes, I took my clothes off for a living, but that in no way entitled men to hurl this constant barrage of abuse at me. Usually I had an answer for everything and would try to put them in their place without causing a scene, often by catching them off-guard with my response.

You might get a guy in front of his mates, laughing at you and asking, 'So what's your degree in, then?'

I would always answer, 'Actually it's a Masters, and it's in Anthropology. What's your Masters in?' They would always look very embarrassed and shut up. Then, just to add insult to injury, I'd add in my poshest home counties accent (very useful, that), 'Not such a smart arse now, are you?' And they'd stop there. Some of the punters assume you only do this job because you're stupid and can do nothing else. They don't even think you can read. But we're easy targets and they're just being pathetic. I can't tell you how many times I've been asked 'Can't you get a proper job?' by a bloke desperate to prove his manhood in front of his friends.

'Whatever for,' I would reply sweetly, 'when I can earn at least twice as much as you do? Anyway, I get to work with such high-calibre men, like you.'

Guys always thought their comments were witty, but you heard the same shit over and over, so after a while you had your sharp comments on tap to cut them dead in their tracks. Of course, there are times where a guy will say things that really get to you that you can't deal with. I remember a guy refusing to pay me once. He was an Essex type who, with his 'look at me' Franck Muller watch and expensive but badly fitted designer suit, thought he was pretty special. We were having the by now usual argument where I was telling him that if he was in the club it was compulsory to put a pound in the jug each time and he kept saying, 'But I don't have to.'

I wanted to say, 'Well that's what compulsory means, you fucking dimwit,' but instead I attempted the diplomatic route and said, 'It's just a pound. I'm only doing my job.'

He got really angry and said, 'I'm fed up with all of you fucking whores coming round begging for money.' He then took twenty pence from his pocket and threw it on the floor saying, 'Go and pick it up off the floor, you horrible bitch.' At this point the one efficient doorman in the club was immediately behind me.

'Look,' I said, 'I'm just trying to do my job and that doesn't include putting up with shit from lowlifes like you. Just put a pound in or leave.'

He refused. 'Fuck off, you skanky whore.' Then he spat in my face. I grabbed the half-empty tumbler from his hand and threw the contents over him, then stormed into the toilets to wipe his saliva from my face. Next thing I knew the manager burst into the changing room; the gay Aussie guy who I'd decided on my first day was an utter wanker. The manager had absolutely no clue what had gone on. He'd just heard the customer's side of the story and reacted.

'You can't behave like that with a customer,' he said.

'What? Did you see what that fucking bastard did to me? He spat at me! Spat!'

'I don't care. You have to pay for his dry cleaning.'

'You're fucking kidding me.'

'I'm not ... Forty quid for the dry cleaning and you're suspended.'

'I'm not giving him a penny. I'd rather quit!'

As it happened, Marie was on that night. On finding out the manager had suspended me she wasn't pleased and wanted to know the whole story. I explained that I had thrown his drink over him, but I did it because he spat in my face. She went mad and said, 'You're not suspended and you're not fucking giving that little fucker a penny for his dry cleaning, I'll 'ave the lot of those bastards out. Get yourself on stage and don't worry about those bunch of wankers and Mark [manager], the fucker, I'll 'ave words with 'im too.'

I actually think Marie hated the customers. But she also didn't like some of the girls and if I'd been one of those I doubt if she'd have come to my aid. I was lucky to be in her good books.

I went on stage a total mess. My face was red from crying and I had washed off my makeup as I'd rubbed hard to clean his filthy spit from my face. I really didn't care, since my night was ruined anyway and I just wanted to get it over with. Situations like this seemed to be happening to me more and more and I was becoming less tolerant of the whole thing.

Even on your best day, carrying that bloody jug means someone will annoy you.

'What's your name?'

'Ellouise.'

'No, your real name.'

Like I'm going to tell you. That's the point of a pseudonym, dumb-arse.

'Where do you live?'

Do they honestly think a girl will ever tell them the truth? Is that how stupid they think we are?

'What's your real job?'

Because surely you can't just be a stripper – shock, horror.

'What charity are you collecting for?'

Goodness, how original! No one's said that before.

'Cheers!' – while clinking their glass on your collection jug, again, highly original.

It doesn't sound so bad but after hearing it several times in a shift you tire of it and wish the ground could swallow you up. Or better still, swallow them up for good.

The other frustration with the jug is people putting in 2p or something equally insulting. A clever stripper knows exactly what goes into her jug; you can hear a pound drop even on the loudest of nights or you have a note on the top of your jug so you can watch what everyone puts in. There are times when a punter has clearly put in a two-pence piece or something but will argue till he's blue in the face that he's put in a pound. You can try to make them pay but usually they ignore you. I was quite persistent so would get it in the end, more out of the principle of the matter than the money itself. You can't catch everyone, though. I've had nuts and bolts, screws, foreign coins, tokens and metal washers put in my jug. I knew that reacting to them was risky but I hated being taken for a fool – and then told to fuck off. As well as guys spitting at you, they might punch, kick, throw a drink over you, burn you with a cigarette or even head-butt you.

I've had it all, apart from the head-butt – but only because I saw it coming and moved fast! I got burned with a cigarette when a guy refused to pay after I told him politely that it was mandatory. He told me to fuck off. I told him if he paid me I would indeed 'fuck off' so he rammed his cigarette into my leg. I screamed and as I ran off he said, 'I knew that would get rid of you, stupid bitch.' Surprise, surprise, he didn't get kicked out so when I went on stage – burnt – he stood in the audience laughing at me. Taking your clothes off after that is really humiliating.

These are the guys that you have to worry about because you don't know what they're capable of. I probably got a bit more shit than most of the girls; firstly because guys thought I was arrogant and needed to be brought down a peg or two, and secondly because I was a smartarse who stood up to them. I always had a sarcastic or sharp comment to hit them with and some guys can't admit defeat from a woman, let alone a stripper. The only thing they can resort to is violence. Sometimes they'll even threaten you with 'I'll 'ave you done'. Or they'll react violently in the club.

On one occasion it began with the usual refusal and 'You're not worth a pound'.

'OK, handsome,' I replied, 'but it's obligatory.'

'Fuck off, you sarcastic bitch.'

'Give me a pound and I'll happily fuck off – your company isn't exactly magnetic.'

Having lost the argument he made a move to head-butt me. I saw it coming and moved but his hand caught me around the back of the neck. His entire pint of Guinness went up in the air and all over me – he hardly had a drop on him – the bouncer saw what was happening and ran in, pulled him off me and sent me away. Of course I'd been collecting because I was due up on stage and I still had to get up there. I was covered in Guinness and had his hand-marks all over my neck and shoulder. The next day I was sore. When I got off stage I was told off.

'Why is it always you, Ellouise?' the manager asked me.

'I'm sorry,' I said. 'I can't be a victim. I have to stand up for my sanity and self-respect.'

He just huffed at me and gave me a warning. Yes, *me*. Not the punter.

And what was a warning supposed to mean? Next time someone calls you an ugly whore, say thank you? That was never going to happen. But a lot of girls did let it happen, and went home crying all the time. Beautiful girls with no confidence because they let these bastards walk all over them. These are the ones who ended up getting excessive cosmetic surgery or became obsessed with dieting; the ones who couldn't cope.

I was coping but I was also getting very stressed in the process. The stupidity of it all was that I was now getting unhappy about being stressed and angry at work. Arguing was not in my nature and here I was arguing on a weekly basis with customers. I'd become a totally different person, but thinking back on it, if I hadn't become that hard person, I don't think I'd have come out of the industry quite so unscathed. Who I *would* be when I came out was another question.

Chapter 19

We can't keep meeting like this

When you feel like shit, you do things to try and make yourself feel better. By my own choice, I had no boyfriend to do that for me and very few friends to share my troubles with. Besides, I wasn't the only stripper with problems. So I decided to do what all girls do when the going gets tough: I went shopping. In fact, I went shopping in style and bought a car, a black Mercedes SLK.

This was a bit out of character for me but it made me feel better and it felt right. This sleek machine was the most luxurious thing I'd ever owned; it was beautiful and did the job of cheering me up in a big way. For months it was my focus; I went to work and found it a little easier to put up with the crap knowing I had my dream car. A few years later I sold it in order to invest in more property but at the time it was just what the doctor ordered. Temporarily happier, I continued to work at both clubs. I was still very close friends with Tamara who was now working at another East End pub – the White Horse – and she seemed to being doing OK. Chantal found out she was pregnant and left, never to be seen again, and Angie had her heart broken by the doorman, met a new guy and emigrated.

Within a few months the excitement of the new car had worn off and I carried on sinking into this pit of misery I'd dug for myself. I decided to take a holiday, thinking if I could just get away and relax I could come back with a clear head. I headed off to the Caribbean to chill out and to sunbathe for two weeks with several books, but all it did was remind me how unhappy I was, how much I hated the job and how I really didn't want to go back. When I returned to England, I took another four or five weeks off. I think I was hoping that if I wished hard enough, something might change in a big way, but it didn't. In any case, the pull of the industry was so strong, I ended up going back. It wasn't fun. I looked around me at the 'girls' who were not far off forty. Some of them had worked for fifteen years and had nothing to show for it – no money, education, family or happiness. I was terrified that I'd end up like them, having to drink every day or take coke just to get through my shifts. I think I knew

I was getting close to my last dance: it would be soon, but I didn't know when.

I did get a new regular, though. He was a young Chinese guy. It always cheers a girl up to get a new regular because as soon as you see them come in you know you're guaranteed money. After a while you can tell them exactly when to come in so it coincides with your quietest shifts. This guy came on a very quiet afternoon; he bought a Coke and made a beeline straight for me. I did back to back dances for him; at least five or six. When I'd finished he bought me a drink and I chatted to him for a while. We didn't get paid for sitdowns but there were no more than ten customers in the pub and I'd danced for five of them. I thought I would chat to this guy and get some more dances out of him since he obviously had cash. We made small talk for twenty minutes.

I can talk about nothing for hours, a trick I learned at Strings, so I chatted, laughed and flirted, then made my excuses, saying, 'I wish I could stay here with you, I'm really enjoying myself, but I'll get in trouble if I'm not working, also they might think you're my boyfriend and boyfriends aren't allowed in.' (The boyfriend bit is always a good touch because it automatically makes him think he could be in my league and be boyfriend material.)

He took the bait and asked me for another dance or six. We were like that for the next two hours: six dances and then a chat in between. The chats were getting shorter each time and I ended up having a very lucrative day. He was also really sweet and not at all lecherous. He was a young guy, quite shy and he hung on to my every word. You could see the adoration in his eyes as he asked me when I would be working again. I told him I had no idea (this was true, I hadn't checked my diary) but all the girls' shifts were on the website so he could find me any time. He did. From that day onwards he came to every single shift I worked. Keep in mind that some of them were lunch shifts, so he was taking afternoons off from work to come in. He bought me chocolates, cashmere scarves, teddies and romantic cards. For a stripper, this is what's known as a desirable customer. Sweet, regular and not too demanding.

It was the same for every shift. He would have six or so dances back to back and then a short chat and so on for the whole shift. On a quiet day that was great but on a packed shift I had to work: when it was busy you danced solidly and could earn £600. I had to explain to him that even though I would much rather spend time with him I had to work. He wasn't happy; he hated seeing me dance for other guys but would still have dances. So he upped his dances to ten, back to back, so he could have me for longer. Generally my shifts would be relatively quiet so to stop me 'having' to dance for other people he would step up his game. When he knew there were other customers I could dance for, he would just have more dances. Sometimes I'd leave him to work the room and he would stare at me intently, getting more and more jealous as time went on.

I could see the jealousy rising and a potential problem brewing on the horizon. You'd think I would have seen it coming and learned my lesson about jealous customers but the money was great and he was genuinely a nice person. Now he began telling customers and bar staff he was my boyfriend; he really did believe he was and he acted like a lovesick teenager. I still didn't see that he posed a threat. It was getting slightly annoying, but these guys soon disappear when they realise that you're never going to go on a date with them. Besides, the kind of money I was earning was too good to turn down. He was giving me at least £150 per shift but sometimes a hell of a lot more.

One day while making small talk I mentioned it was my mum's birthday. It was what I considered general time-filling chit-chat. I said that I wasn't sure what to get her and that I was considering taking her to the theatre. It was idle talk but of course he took it seriously. The next day, he came in with theatre tickets for my mum and me – and him! I thanked him but all the while I was desperately thinking of an excuse I could use to get out of this one. He went on about being excited to meet my mum, etc. That's when the guilt kicks in. You feel like you're leading these guys on and scamming them, when really they are free agents and you've given them no clear indication that you'll ever go out with them. On various occasions I had told him that I couldn't see him outside of work. He'd asked me to his work party once and I made it clear to him that I just couldn't do that.

Under the circumstances it was inevitable that he would soon become insanely jealous. And, boy, did he! If I was over-talkative to any customers or spoke with the manager for too long he would pull me up on it. He'd already informed everyone he was my boyfriend. A group of regulars who came in every day for a pint would tease the hell out of me, knowing he was just a nutter, but it was getting really irritating. It was basically like being in a bad relationship. I got out of the theatre trip using some lame excuse. I think it was something like my mum's partner had organised a surprise party, family only, and very much a quiet night. (Just in case he was expecting an invite.) I apologised profusely about the wasted theatre tickets and offered to ask around if anyone wanted to buy them, but he said he would take work colleagues. At least that was over, but I could see he wasn't very happy.

His next move was asking to walk me to my car. My reaction was to tell him I didn't have a car and would get a cab home, just to cover my back. I knew the next question would be, 'Can I wait with you while you get your cab?' I went on to tell him how the club rules are that the doorman has to see us to our cabs for safety. With another disastrous situation averted we made small talk about how I planned to get a car and cabs were too expensive blah, blah, blah. So we carried on with the night as per usual, with him having large amounts of dances, and me chatting rubbish. A week later he came in and told me he had bought a car so I wouldn't have to waste money on cabs any more and he could drive me anywhere.

That was the final straw. It was more hassle than it was worth. Not only was he embarrassing me by telling everyone he was my boyfriend, he was constantly telling me off for speaking to other people and having tantrums when I spent too long with another customer. I'd had two or three months of this every day and I couldn't bear it any more, I'd told him time and time again that I wasn't his girlfriend and could never see him outside of work but it went in one ear and out the other. So in the end I had to sit him down and 'break up' with him. I thought if I did it like we were actually having the fantasy relationship that he had in his head he might understand it better.

I sat him down and began.

'I don't think we should see each other any more. I just don't think we're suited and it would be best if we split up. I don't want a relationship.'

He was devastated, but for the first time it actually went in. It was as if all the other times I'd said it to him as a customer didn't exist or he hadn't heard them. I told him it would be better if he didn't come in any more as I thought it best we didn't see each other. He was heartbroken.

'I love you, Ellouise. We were getting on so well. I know I can be jealous but …'

I sent him home feeling really terrible on his behalf. I wasn't proud of what had happened and I wasn't happy that everyone in the pub saw it as the end to a very funny story: I just saw a devastated man who felt like shit because of me. He came in on my next shift. I saw him before he saw me and hid behind the bar. I asked the manager to go and speak to him. 'Tell him I'm off sick and that he shouldn't probably come in any more.' I should've faced him myself but I couldn't take any more. Eventually he stopped coming to the club.

A lot of girls would have just kept it going, I was

sacrificing a lot of money by losing him, but most girls will take everything they can. I know so many girls who lead guys on, telling them they will go out with them as soon as they can get free of their work or their university exams. They'll say that they will definitely go out in four or five weeks, even to the point of making plans with the guy for dinner, a show, whatever.

Then she'll say, 'I can't wait five weeks to see you, but I have to concentrate on my thesis/exams/sick grandma [whatever the chosen delaying tactic], please come in and see me.' She will then set up a date with him, on her next quiet shift, telling him to come in on a certain day where it will be really quiet and they'll have the chance 'to talk'. Suddenly she has this guy popping in when she wants him to. He'll keep coming in for however many weeks, thinking there's a date in the offing while she flirts and talks about their plans for the big date. At some point she'll say, very sadly, 'I really wish I could just stay with you, but I have to work,' and that's how he starts spending money. Voilà! The perfect recipe for one regular!

When the date comes round, she will either keep delaying, saying she didn't finish her thesis in time/her nan's still sick, so can he please wait a few more weeks? Of course she's been *so* looking forward to their date; God, she *needs* it being so stressed out and all. Some girls know the guy won't buy it so they just blow him off. Others actually do see their regulars once in a while outside work to keep them coming in. It might be a monthly dinner date or more in some cases. I was once sat in a restaurant with a bunch of girls from work when another girl walked in with her regular on her arm. She almost died when she realised four girls she worked with were there, had seen her and were all whispering and giggling round the table. A few girls – not many – admit to having monthly lunches with their regulars to keep them, and some girls are clearly shagging their regulars, but keep them coming in for extra cash.

Chapter 20

∞

Textual harassment

One morning I got a call from a guy I'd gone out with briefly in my Strings days.

'You know that girl that hates you? Jane? Well I was in a club last night and she was fucked, out of her brain. She was all over me, saying we should go out and fuck. She kept mentioning you and saying she hated you and thought we should get together to piss you off.'

Hmm, that was interesting, if not exactly what you want to hear. He'd spoken to one of my other friends first before calling me, just to check out whether he should tell me. This girl had gone on to tell someone else, so eventually she found out that I knew. I was slightly embarrassed as I felt bad for Jane: she was a bitch and made my life hell, but this was something I should probably keep to myself. But I didn't lose sleep over it. Anyway, he didn't have sex with her. He got one of her mates to put her in a cab home.

When she found out that word had got out about what she'd done, she did what Jane always did: found something she could hit me with in return. This time she told a few of my big-spending regulars that I was married with kids and I was taking the piss out of them. Luckily some of these guys just laughed at her as they were older and wiser and knew what the industry was all about. One or two did avoid me from then on, but it didn't change my earnings – there was always someone right behind them.

From this point on I felt sorry for her more than anything. She was a really mixed-up girl, given that she was willing to go to any extent just to affect my life. I haven't seen her for years now and she still asks my friends 'What's that bitch doing?' or 'Are you still friends with that cow?' You'd think that after five years she'd get over it but no, she's like a small dog with a bone.

You're probably thinking, 'Well Ellouise, if things were that bad why didn't you just leave and work somewhere else?' Fair enough. I suppose it might sound to some people like the simplest thing to do. But actually it's very, very hard. As I've said, for good or bad, the industry sucked you in and when you were earning good money and having a laugh with your mates it was brilliant. For every customer who harassed you and abused you there were usually twenty to heap compliments on you. All of that makes it very hard to turn your back. And besides, I wasn't ready to leave the industry yet, so it would be more hassle going to look for another place to work, getting new customers and making new friends. There would probably be late nights and intimate lap-dancing as well, something I didn't want.

The gay Aussie manager decided to leave – can't say I wasn't glad to see the back of him – and that only left one manager, Philip, who had a girlfriend of a couple of years, but shagged innumerable strippers when she wasn't around. To run both clubs you need two managers at least, so they soon employed another guy called Greg. He and I got on really well. He wanted to buy a property so I told him about my mortgage and we would always have a little chat. He had a girlfriend, an air hostess, but within weeks of him starting the job she couldn't handle it and gave him an ultimatum. He chose to stick with the job so they broke up.

It turned out that I knew some of his friends: his best mate's girlfriend was an acquaintance of mine so we would always have something to talk about and I saw him out once or twice. It doesn't take Sherlock Holmes to see where this was going. I didn't really like him – not like that, anyway – but he was a really nice guy and paid me a lot of attention. I was pretty fragile and unhappy, so when he asked me out I accepted, on strict instructions that no one was to know. I knew our working together would make it an issue so I asked him not to tell anyone, which he was happy with as he didn't want to get into trouble: all the bosses are warned to stay away from the dancers when they first start. (I think just about every manager ends up shagging at least one stripper, with the exception of the gay manager, but rumour had it he shagged a few customers!)

We dated casually and everything was fine. Neither one of us had time for much more as we both worked a full shift load. I preferred it like that; it was almost a control thing on my part. But mentally it was really good for me to have him around. I needed someone who could be close to me, so I could blow off steam when I was stressed and upset. The fact that he worked in the industry and understood was a bonus. In truth what I probably needed at the time was a real friend, not a partner.

We'd been going out for a few months when he took me away for the weekend. He checked when I had no shifts planned and organised a weekend in the country, hoping it would cheer me up. As we were both off work at the same time, people put two and two together and Marie found out. Only one or two members of staff knew – none of the girls – but I was pretty pissed off and he was scared Marie would sack him. Surprisingly, she was over the moon. She went on about how I was one of her favourite girls and that she couldn't be happier. When he heard that he wanted to tell everyone, but I put my foot down and made him keep it a secret. In hindsight I should have looked at why I wanted secrecy and seen that I didn't really have the right feelings for him: it was more a relationship of convenience and fulfilled a need I had to be loved. It was totally selfish but at the time I didn't realise what I was doing. He was falling in love with me but all I knew was that I was happy.

After we'd been seeing each other for about six months, everyone found out and that's when things went slightly sour for me. It was rocket fuel for my enemies and girls who'd never uttered a word to him before were suddenly all over him like a rash. It was all done to irritate me but it didn't really work. In fact I really didn't care, which should have told me my feelings for him weren't *those* sorts of feelings. I should have left him, not because of the girls trying to wind me up, but because I wasn't into him enough for it to be worth the trouble. But then I got a new stalker and had other things to think about.

'I'm going to do you, you stripper bitch.'

'Who do you think you are, you stripper whore?'

These were the first two text messages. I thought maybe it was a joke or something, even though they were not exactly funny messages.

I tried calling the phone and just got voicemail so I left a message.

'I got some texts from this number. I don't know who you are but seeing as you know my number, call me back so we can find out what the problem is.'

Of course I didn't get a reply. Part of me was hoping that someone had just got a wrong number, but the 'stripper bitch' reference was pretty clear. I got regular texts from this person, ranging from 'Who do you think you are, you're nothing but a whore' to 'I'm gonna fuck you up, you stripper bitch'.

I tried to call the phone from various different numbers but it never rang. It went straight to voicemail, so they were obviously just using the number to harass me. The messages kept coming. There were at least three or four a day, sometimes five, all in a row, and the content was getting nastier.

'I'm gonna scar your face for life. Think you're so

pretty now.' This was their favourite: threatening to scar my face. They'd just change the order of words.

'Wait till you see how pretty you are when I'm done with your face. I'm gonna fuck up your face, then we'll see how pretty you are bitch.'

I was terrified, more than I'd ever been before. I was constantly jumpy and wouldn't walk to my car alone. I still didn't change my number at first as I hoped it would go away. And me being me my first thought was defiant. Why the hell should I change my number? It would just show I'm scared – which I was. The most frightening thing was that I had no idea who was sending the messages. I had an idea that it might be Jane; she was the only person who really hated me but as horrible as she was, I didn't want to believe she was capable of this.

I was due to go on holiday with Tamara the next day. We were taking a well-earned girly holiday to Mexico. The messages continued, but now there was a slight shift in content.

'You think you're so clever. Well who's clever now? I just grassed you up to the taxman.'

Instead of worrying me this was a slight relief as it crossed out anybody too close to me. A lot of girls don't pay tax and never have, but I had an accountant and was square with mine. I could never have got a mortgage otherwise. I left for the airport with Tamara in the morning, left a message for my accountant warning him of the threat, switched my phone off and did my best to put it out of my mind. I was determined to enjoy this holiday.

On arriving in Mexico I turned my phone on for five minutes. Stupid mistake. I should have just had it off all week, but I wanted to stay in touch with my mum. There was a message I didn't want.

'I hope your plane crashes and you die.'

I was in tears. I realised I was dealing with something really serious and also had to face the prospect that it was probably someone from work. Who else could have known I was on holiday, right down to the day I was flying? After that I didn't turn my phone on for the rest of the holiday, although the stalker was always at the back of my mind.

When we got back to the UK, almost immediately I received a barrage of texts. There were around half a dozen in all, saying how they were going to 'fuck up my face', 'scar me for life' and 'change my life for ever'. I phoned Greg, who came straight round and we went to the police. I would have gone alone but I was petrified to leave the house by myself. The police took it pretty seriously. I was taken to an interview room and asked to start the story from the beginning. Luckily I had kept over half the texts, all of the really bad ones anyway. While we were sitting there the texts kept coming in – there were about seven during the half-hour interview – so they realised the seriousness of the situation. They told me this kind of thing was a grey issue with the law right now and there was not a huge amount they could do unless the person actually harmed me (I believe the law has since changed). I was so incensed. I remember sobbing and saying to the police, 'Well thank you. When she kills me or scars my face for life [I was sure it was a she] you can help me.' The incident with the taxi driver who'd tried to run me over meant I already had little faith in the legal system. The police said there were things they could do but just couldn't make an arrest as the person wasn't effectively breaking the law. Yet.

In fairness, they did their best. The case went straight to the CID. They put the number on trace and had regular contact with me. They went to my work to tell them of the situation and warned them to be alert. They also went to the place where I lived, which was one of those new developments with a concierge, and instructed them to keep a watch for anyone hanging around or anything unusual.

The texts kept coming. I now had a doorman walk me to my car every night. Then I'd get into my car quickly and lock the door, after which I would sit there petrified. The first night it happened, a text came through straight away.

'Scared? Need a bodyguard?'

I began to shake. I looked around and could see no one but it didn't matter since they were obviously watching me. I was so scared that when I got back to my flat I asked the porter to see me into my building. He knew the score from the police and was more than happy to help. From now on, whenever I came in late, he told me to drive to the estate office and someone would see me up to my door.

A few days later, after leaving a middle shift, I went to my car alone. It was 7pm and still light out. When I'd arrived I'd found a parking space a twenty-second walk from the club and thought I would be fine. As soon as I got in my car the text came.

'Feeling brave tonight – no escort. We'll see how long that lasts.'

I drove straight to the police station. This was getting out of control. How long could it go on for? I waited there for about two hours until the guy from the CID could see me. I showed him the texts which proved how closely this person was watching me. The guy from the CID took some notes and said they would visit me tomorrow.

They came bright and early. (Strippers don't usually

rise till way after 10am.) They'd traced the calls back to an unregistered pay-as-you-go chip. All they knew was that it was on Virgin, and bought as a chip not as a phone package. They advised me to change jobs and stay with friends or family until this had all calmed down (or I was dead). They told me to change my phone number straight away and give no one the new number. I had to leave my job and home, have no contact with my friends and family and hope the person who wanted to kill me got bored!

I refused to leave my flat or job. I wasn't going to let this person win. Deep down I was pretty sure it was a dancer or linked to work in some way and by leaving I would be admitting defeat. I did change my number, and gave it to only four people: my mum, my partner, Tamara and Melissa. The messages stopped. At first this scared me even more. What if they were looking for new ways to scare me? It was ages before I would go anywhere alone. I made the doorman see me to my car for a few months after that and was jumpy and nervous for ages.

This had to be the single most scary thing that has ever happened to me, simply because I had no idea who was doing it. Once things eventually calmed down I took a fortnight off work. When I returned, slightly rested but still unhappy, I knew I still didn't love Greg, but I needed him. I was struggling to cope with things and needed some security, and he was such a nice guy. It was almost as if I was trying to force myself to love him, when really I should have been looking elsewhere for a solution to my unhappiness.

Chapter 21

❧

Those aren't your pockets, are they?

I told myself that at least at Diamonds, I knew everything there was to know. I knew all the regulars: there were some that would use it as their local pub and were just friendly guys who didn't have dances, always sat in 'their' spot at the back of the bar and would buy you a drink if you felt like you needed one. When I returned to work some new girls had started. They were lively and fun and seemed to enjoy a good laugh, which was exactly what I needed to lighten my mood. On my first night back they got one at my expense.

You get some strange things happen during dances and this night I was doing a private dance for a guy when he wet himself mid-dance. He was really drunk and when he sat down, he was so wasted he must have just been in a very confused state. Luckily we didn't do actual lap-dancing at Diamonds (can you imagine?) so I was a fair distance from him. It actually wasn't until a girl dancing opposite pointed it out that I realised and within seconds every girl in the room had the giggles.

'Ha, ha, you made a customer piss himself!'

'What?'

'Your customer. Look, he's pissed himself.'

I rushed out, got the doorman and left him to deal with it – revenge for all of the times those guys on the door had left me in the lurch. The girls got a big laugh out of it all night, more at me than at the poor customer. It might sound unnecessarily cruel to giggle (but you would have too, I bet) but customers are always doing idiotic or just damn awful things during dances – it's probably the same tossers that give you shit during your jug – so I think it's fair that we girls are allowed to laugh at them when they make absolute dicks of themselves. Some of the things guys do during a dance are pretty bizarre. For example they'll be as lively as hell when they're out on the floor, however, as soon as they sit down they will fall asleep. The girl will pretend to keep going with the dance but in reality she's just standing there having a laugh with her friends. You can always bet that one guy will fall asleep and spill his drink all over his crotch. It doesn't always wake them up but when the girl shakes him awake he walks out slightly confused with a big wet patch which everyone sees well before he does.

A lot of the time the girls will play games with the guys just for their own amusement. At least 75 per cent of the time during a double dance (two girls, two guys) guys will ask you to kiss each other – the old girl-on-girl thing. Melissa and I would always do what they did in the movie *American Pie*.

'We'll kiss if you guys go first,' we'd tell them.

The number of guys who will snog their mate after a few drinks in the hope of getting two girls to do it is amazing. We would just laugh at them and say we were kidding and they would take it in good humour. However there are some guys whose idea of fun and games during a dance is a bit different. Usually you do a dance and the guy compliments you and slips you his business card or asks you to dance for his mate. Dance over. It's simple and sweet and everyone's happy. But you always get the odd guy who ruins it for everyone. Firstly – and thank God this doesn't happen too often – you'll get the guy who decides to flash at you. This has only happened twice to me in my entire stripping career: both times it was at Diamonds.

The first was during a dance where two of us were doing a dance for one guy. This guy got his tiny little penis out (and I'm not just saying that: it was tiny) and just sat there. The other girl saw it first and started laughing so much. I had no idea what was going on and when I saw what was happening I burst into hysterics. He just adjusted himself and ran out. We both stood there laughing so hard until we cried. For the rest of the shift we couldn't look each other in the eye in case it set us off laughing again.

The other time I was flashed couldn't have been more different. I had my back turned to the guy I was dancing for when he started to stand. I saw him pull his penis out and had no idea what was going on but as soon as I saw the situation, I jumped off the platform. He went to cover himself up and I kicked him really hard in the bum. Then I screamed for the bouncer and as the guy started to move, I grabbed his hair so he couldn't get away. The bouncer ran in and on seeing me with the guy's hair and him still exposed, looked slightly shocked but took over and threw him out. The reason I reacted so strongly was because he had started to get up off his seat which meant he could have grabbed me and tried to rape me.

This is an extreme, but something similar happened to a friend of mine at another big West End club. She'd been doing a lap-dance for a guy and when she turned her back to wriggle her bum in his face he'd pulled his penis out, grabbed her and pulled her down on to his lap. He hadn't managed to force himself into her but only because she screamed and struggled, but she felt it against her, pushing into her skin and realised what was happening. She had a lucky escape but she didn't dance for months after that; it really fucked her up. She wanted to call the police and have him done for attempted rape but the club wouldn't let her because they didn't want the bad press. Needless to say she didn't go back to work there again.

Another thing guys do during dances is touch themselves. It happens in every club. The guys are very discreet but you can still see them doing it. They have both hands in their pockets and when they think you're not looking, they start rubbing themselves. Some guys will actually cut through their pockets so they can have a full wank when you're dancing. Of course they think you don't know, but a stripper's job is to always be aware of what's going on with her customer. There's not a lot you can do to stop this behaviour. You can ask them to 'sit still' or if they play dumb and carry on you can ask them to take their hands out of their pockets. Most girls turned a blind eye but I always made sure they knew that I knew. Nevertheless, it didn't stop them.

There was one guy who would regularly have dances with me and a Brazilian girl called Christie. One day I said to her, 'I'm sure he keeps touching himself every time I turn my back.'

She decided to look out for it although she wasn't so sure. Next time I did a dance, she peeked through the curtain to watch. Sure enough, every time I turned around he would rub his penis. After the dance she confirmed what I thought and we told him we wouldn't dance for him any more. Whether or not the other girls did was up to them but we weren't interested. He gave us both the creeps anyway so it was good riddance. We were pleased when he stopped coming in until one day, about a year later, a new Russian girl introduced me to her husband. It was him, the jerk-off guy.

He started coming to pick her up at the end of her shift, but instead of waiting outside like other partners, he would come in and stand right at the front of the stage watching the girls. She never had a problem with him doing this but the management did and the girls hated it. Everyone knew about him and it put us in a really uncomfortable position to have this girl's husband put a pound in our jug and stand right at the front watching – actually he was leering. Don't get me wrong: boyfriends would come to pick up the girls from time to time, but they generally wouldn't watch the girls. They'd either have a drink at the bar or play the fruit machine. It was kind of like an unwritten code where we all felt it was more respectful to their partners as well as to the rest of us. After a while the jerk-off guy was told he had to stay off the premises.

Meanwhile a stunning Brazilian girl joined us. Her name was Mona and she was beautiful but turned out to be one of the most conniving girls I've met. She was a prime example of how being ugly inside can detract from outer beauty. From the beginning she caused trouble. At first it happened between her and the other Brazilian girls. She told lies about their boyfriends trying it on with her and generally pissed them off. A few of the Brazilians I was friendly with said she was a troublemaker. From what I could see she thought everyone fancied her and was addicted to attention but seemed harmless otherwise. I stayed neutral, until she began to annoy me when she became fixated on Greg. I wasn't too bothered at first. She'd follow him around, to the basement, and constantly hassle him. He would reject her time and time again. Then she started telling people that it was the other way around and that he was obsessed with her. She'd get drunk and start begging him to be with her. On one occasion she tried to give him money, telling him she wanted him to have a present from her.

Greg decided to have a word with one of the bar staff, a Colombian girl who was a friend of hers. He asked her to tell Mona to leave him alone. Now I was pissed off, mainly as I felt she was being openly disrespectful to me. We had a lot of rows, not just over Greg but because she'd tell my friends stories about us that just weren't true. She was a pathological liar and her high and whiny voice was an extra irritant.

The Mona situation didn't go on for too long. Already that year I'd put up with far too much to let a silly young girl mess with my head. When she made quiet comments in the changing room about me I'd turn around and scream at her to stand in front of me and say it to my face. She never did; instead she just turned and ran out. Sometimes I'd just confront her in front of everyone in the changing room, knowing that she'd lied to a few people in that room so she couldn't deny it. My attitude gained me the respect of the other Brazilian girls, which is a hard thing to do! The thing about her was she had a boyfriend who the others said was a lovely guy. He would wait outside to pick her up. Apparently even he'd been warned about her by the Brazilian girls but he stuck by her and the next thing we knew, she was pregnant. I was relieved because it meant she would leave me alone. Since I'd begun directly approaching her she had quietened down a bit. (I always approached her in front of a room full of people so she couldn't change my words and spread lies about me.) Hopefully now that she was happily pregnant it would distract her from being a minx and make her grow up a bit.

One afternoon I was working a double with her and another Brazilian girl, a very quiet girl called Jenni. We were at Pearls and going on to Diamonds so we got into a cab together.

Mona, Jenni and I were in the cab and they were doing most of the talking – when the conversation turned to babies.

'What do you think of my baby?' asked Mona.

'I think it'll be wonderful for you,' I replied.

I knew she wanted an argument but I didn't want to give it to her. I let her and Jenni carry on talking until Mona asked me, 'So why aren't you having babies?'

I wasn't sure where all of this was going but I knew she wasn't just being friendly all of a sudden.

'I will, but not while I'm a stripper,' I said. 'I want a normal life before having any.' I wasn't having a dig at her; it was just my personal preference. The cab arrived at Pearls and we went inside but Mona didn't come down to change. Within minutes, the manager, Phil, came running downstairs and asked why I'd been shouting at Mona in the cab.

'What are you talking about, Phil? There was no shouting.'

'She said you told her it was wrong to have kids if you're a stripper.'

I laughed. 'What the fuck has she been saying?' Mona was behind him, crying and holding on to her totally flat stomach as if she'd been violated in some way. I turned to Jenni who was also changing.

'Tell the truth about everything that was said in the cab,' I said to her. I walked away and carried on changing. Phil hadn't even thought to check out the story with Jenni and Mona had assumed Jenni would back her up. She hadn't banked on Jenni telling the truth.

Phil apologised to me but I never even turned to acknowledge his apology. The fact that I'd worked there for four years didn't matter: he'd believed a stupid little girl's version of the story. As soon as he left I blew up and screamed at her. I just went mad; I don't even remember what I said. I just remember a new girl coming in to see me having a screaming row with Mona. I ended up good friends with her and we still laugh about the fact that this was the first impression she had of me. Not good. After that the only thing Mona ever said to me was, 'How do you know it's not Greg's baby? It might be.'

I didn't even bother replying, just smiled. I knew she was a pathological liar and I never doubted him. I told him and he went mad. She eventually left to have the baby but returned to work as soon as she got her figure back. I was long gone by that time so she would never bother me again. I think this whole episode marked a bit of a watershed. I'd been feeling fed up with stripping for some time but now I'd fallen out of favour with Marie, who decided I was a troublemaker and that my relationship with Greg was now a problem for her and the club – just like that. You didn't ever want to be in her bad books, but here I was. Girls who fell out with Marie didn't last long at Diamonds and Pearls. She made life so difficult for them they had to leave. Or she sacked them. I knew my days working for her were numbered but I didn't know just what number I was up to.

Marie decided I was no good for Greg and told him I clearly didn't love him. I did love him, but just as a friend, and we got on really well. We were happy together but I just knew he wasn't the one for me. I think – well, I now know – that the only reason I stayed in the relationship so long was because I was so stressed and needed someone. Not to mention the fact that every time I considered breaking up with him some drama would happen in my life and the time was never right. Marie didn't know this – she only dealt in black and white – and now that she'd decided I was trouble, she went out of her way to make my life difficult. The good times and the fun with the girls were increasingly outweighed by all the bad things that were going on. Although I was reluctant to admit it to myself I hated the job and seemed to be in a cycle of two steps forward, one step back. As you know, whether you're in a crap job or a rubbish relationship, admitting the problem to yourself is one thing; doing something about it is something else entirely.

Meanwhile another customer had tried to follow me home. He'd left the club about two hours before I finished and sat in his car. The doorman had seen him and kept an eye on him, thinking perhaps he'd just had a bit too much and was sleeping for a few hours before driving home (not unusual). I finished work, got in my car and drove off. As he started his car and began to follow me without turning on his lights, the doorman went straight in to call the manager, who immediately called me and asked if I was being followed.

'There's a guy a bit further back with no lights on who's been there for a while.' They told me to head back to the club but not to make any sudden u-turns; in other words, drive in a loop but head back, so I did. I lured him almost all the way to the club, but a street away he caught on and fled.

I had no idea how much more I could take. I was constantly crying and I hated myself. Not for the dancing but for who I had to be to do it: hard, bitchy and cold. I knew I needed to change things soon, but what else was I qualified to do? I'd been a stripper for almost a decade, which didn't really give me much to put on my CV. And even if I did get a job I wasn't ready to adapt to a life of getting up at the crack of dawn, just to earn 18 grand a year in some McJob. I wouldn't earn much more, not with my CV …

Name:	Ellouise – Ellie – Elle – Ali
Work experience:	Strings – 3 years
	Glamour model – 4 years
	Diamonds – 3½ years

So I just kept on going, getting more and more depressed, arguing with customers then driving home every night crying. And it was the best thing that could have happened to me. I got so low, I started to realise it wasn't even worth the money. One night, red-eyed and exhausted, I set myself a goal. I'd sell my car, sell some of my possessions, save a bit more money and leave. For good. I'd start again and do anything. The next day I put my car on the market, took fewer shifts and arranged to go to Peru to do a walk for charity. I had to banish this selfish, greedy, aggressive person I'd become. I wanted to be the girl I was before, the girl who never raised her voice or lost her temper, no matter how bad things were.

Chapter 22

❦

No good in goodbye

The phone call came. My father was dying. I hadn't seen him for over ten years and hoped never to see him again, but I was told it was a matter of days and he wanted to see me.

The call had come at work so I just got my stuff and walked out without asking permission. People called me back, but I just kept walking. There was a lovely barmaid called Debs who was worried about me getting into trouble so she called Greg. He called me and all I could say was, 'My dad's about to die; he's got a few days left and wants to see me. I've got to go,' and hung up. He explained my absence, got someone to cover his shift and came to my flat.

I was in shock, not because my father was dying but because I had to confront my feelings for a man who made my life hard. It also meant I had to see my sister and my dad's wife, a painful reminder of my teenage years. The next day I went to see him. But he didn't want to see me to apologise. I didn't hear the word 'sorry' once. It was all about him; he just wanted to make peace with himself before meeting his maker. I was devastated and went out and got so drunk that I was sick for two days. Then, almost on autopilot, I went to the hospital most days until he died. Apparently he had had cancer in several places. He'd had radiotherapy and the hospital had hoped for a good result but he wouldn't stop drinking until the day he was admitted to the hospital.

I was called in his final moments: he'd had a stroke, two small heart attacks and had developed septicaemia, and it was a case of what was going to kill him first. The doctors begged to speak with me in private as the family – his wife and my sister – had refused to put him on DNR (do not resuscitate). I was shocked and the doctors were happy that they'd found a family member who would listen to reason. I wasn't in a position to make the decision so I sat his wife down, made her look at him and said, 'You're being fucking selfish. There's nothing left of him and you have no right to keep him alive for your own reasons.'

She broke down. 'I don't want him to leave but you're right.'

To the relief of the doctor, she agreed to the DNR. I was shocked, firstly because I didn't think she loved him quite so much and secondly because I thought anything I said would be ignored. By the time he died, he couldn't recognise anyone and was in great pain. If one thing came out of me having to go there and revisit bad memories, it's that I did something positive and let him die. Still I couldn't get over the fact that he wanted me there just to ease his own conscience. People ask me now how I stayed there so long. Why was I at his bedside instead of just leaving as soon as I'd done my duty? I guess I wanted to hear him apologise for what he did to me – and to Mum – and I clung on to the vain and stupid hope that he would.

But he didn't.

I was in more of a mess than I knew. Being me, I thought I was coping well but I was hardly eating and became very, very thin. I went to the doctor and told him my dad had just died.

'I've barely eaten for ten days. Everything I force down I throw up.'

He said there was nothing he could do. It was all part of grief. You could see my ribs and I just looked a mess. At the same time I was trying so hard to make myself love Greg: I wanted to banish my demons and prove to myself that I didn't have commitment issues, but in truth it was all too much for me. I ended up doing what I often did when I had no idea where to turn. I went back to work. I needed to be around familiar faces. Straight away Marie told me I looked no good, was too skinny and needed to put some weight on. I was still in her bad books and the fact that my dad had died two weeks before didn't lessen that fact. She wanted to see Greg and me split up and she wanted me gone.

It was the month before Christmas, the busiest time of year but also the most stressful. This was the time you earned the big cash, when every club, from one end of the country to another, is packed with men spending like the world was about to end. This was one of those times when you saw men at their very worst: very pissed, very rude and with not a care in the world, especially not for you. But if you want to make real money, this is the time to do it. I convinced myself I had to do it. My confidence was really low and all the weight loss meant I was skeletal and my boobs had totally disappeared.

I remember having a few arguments; my nerves were pretty frayed and a guy made a nasty comment so I told him where to go. We had a huge row and Donnie told me if I had one more argument I'd be in big trouble. That meant that I wasn't allowed to defend myself. A few days later, I was collecting my jug and one of my regulars put twenty quid in for him and his two mates. We were having a laugh and I pointed my finger at him saying, 'Does your wife know you're giving me her Christmas shopping money?' Donnie grabbed my arm, pulled me out of their circle and started shouting at me in front all of the customers.

'You're fucking trouble, Ellouise! I've had enough of you; you're a fucking waste of time!'

I burst into tears while the customers stepped in to back me up. When he realised his mistake, he didn't bother apologising but just screamed at me to go on stage now and then get changed and go home. I still had five minutes to collect but he made the DJ put me on early, not even allowing me to wipe the tears from my eyes. It was so embarrassing having to stand in front of a sixty-strong crowd with a fake smile, stripping, with tears running down my face. But that's exactly why he did it. The next day I woke up not knowing if I'd been sacked or not. I phoned in and everything was fine. Except me. It was about a week before Christmas and I went into my shift at the Pearls on the verge of a breakdown.

Henry was there. He was a customer who'd become quite a good friend over the past four years. I would burden him with all of my problems and he would laugh at me and try to cheer me up. He'd always chat with me and enjoyed my company over and above having a dance, even though more often than not I was depressed. He knew about my dad and he knew about the situation with the owners pushing me to quit. I don't think they wanted to sack me because they thought Greg might leave and they didn't want to lose him. Usually I tell customers very little about my life but Henry and I had been sounding boards for each other over the years and had a good friendship.

'Just leave, Ellouise. You know you have to.'

'Oh, I don't know, Henry. I don't know what to do any more.'

Of course you do Ellouise. You've been thinking about it for too long now.'

'I still want to save up more money and I'm thinking about having a boob job, so perhaps I'll leave after I've earned the money for that.'

'Listen Ellouise. I know how unhappy you are here, and I know that your confidence has gone since you lost weight and your breasts disappeared. So here's the thing. If I give you a Christmas present of the money for a boob job will you leave here and promise never to work here again? Dance if you want, but never come back here.'

'I can't take money from you, Henry. I don't need it, honestly.'

He was determined to give it to me. 'Ellouise, in all the years you've known me you've never tried to wheedle money out of me – and I'm a very rich man. Please take it. It's for me, too. I'll feel like I've done something worthwhile and at least I'll know I've bought you a Christmas present you want.'

And with that he took out his chequebook and wrote me a cheque for three thousand pounds.

'Cash it only if you leave.' He pressed it into my hand and told me to put it somewhere safe. I worked the rest of my shift and when I was going round with my jug and a guy grabbed my ass so hard he left red marks, I needed little incentive to move on. I finished my shift, still unsure about the cheque and leaving for good. When I woke in the morning I decided to cancel all of my shifts and take two weeks off, to think about my life, grieve for my dad – and the life I'd lost – and gain some weight. I hadn't decided if I'd come back.

When I called in and started cancelling my shifts, Marie grabbed the phone from the office girl and snarled, 'If you take time off, you ain't comin' back.'

I told her I needed a break but she wasn't having it. I was furious and felt like my head was about to burst so I said, 'Stick your piece-of-shit job. I wasn't planning to come back anyway.' She never realised it, but she did me a favour.

That was one of the happiest days in my life. An overwhelming sense of relief and freedom came over me. I phoned my friend Marianne who'd had one of the best boob jobs I'd seen and she booked me in with her surgeon in Stockholm for the middle of January. Within days the other girls were calling me. Apparently Marie had been telling them how she got rid of 'that fucking bitch' and telling Greg to do the same.

Several people – girls I trusted – then told me how Greg just stood there while she called me a worthless bitch and never said a word. Apparently he just laughed when everyone else laughed (there were people who were very happy to see the back of me). I confronted him and we had a huge argument. It was to be our last one. There was nothing left between us any more. When I told him it wasn't working he said he was heartbroken. As soon as he went back to the club Marie said, 'See, that's what she's like; I bet she's cheating on you.' We tried to talk over the next few days but it didn't work. He wanted to patch things up, but at the same time he ended up getting drunk and snogging one of the girls in a club after work. He begged for forgiveness but there was nothing left to forgive: we were in tatters.

So that was Diamonds. I have a few friends who still work there but I have never been near that place since, and never wish to. If anything happens to me when this book comes out then that's where to look for clues. I will be watching my back for years.

A month or two after I left, Melissa was sacked. They blamed her for telling me about Greg kissing someone else but Marie wanted her out anyway. I felt really bad, but although Melissa didn't realise it, leaving that place would be a big step forward for her too.

Chapter 23

❧

Don't save the last dance for me

Months later and armed with a new set of boobs, I still wasn't dancing. It had now been over four months since I'd left and I was feeling almost like my old self. For the first time in years, I felt I'd fully taken control of my life and I could feel the aggression, stress and greed leaving me. I knew I couldn't do nothing for ever, so I went back to dancing, but this time as a very different person: older, stronger, confident, in control and self-aware. Or so I thought.

Tamara worked at the White Horse; it was a pub, not far from Diamonds but very different. There was no private dancing, just stage shows. Now given that I didn't really like stage dancing this might not seem like a good choice, but I didn't want a place that would take over my life. Here you could only work a maximum of three shifts a week and the money was a lot less than I was used to. But that suited me perfectly. I didn't want to get so engrossed in money and earning enough to keep things ticking over suited me perfectly. I planned to do the odd extra shift here and there if things were tight. While I had savings, I'd planned to buy another property so dipping into my nest egg was out of the question.

I also knew half of the girls who worked there and within a week of me starting Melissa joined as well. I was nervous on my first day. This is going to sound a little contradictory but having a new set of boobs made me feel shy about getting them out. Sue, the owner, put me on with Tamara for my first shift. It was a busy night and I had a brilliant night. Usually when I say this it means I've earned a lot of money, but for once I mean it in the sense that I actually enjoyed myself. Everyone was so nice: it was a really close-knit group of DJs, bar staff, managers and girls. Everyone seemed friendly and mixed well together. Not having private dancing meant there was far less competition between the girls. Of course there was some bitchiness: it wouldn't be a strip club without it.

I loved it here and realised that being treated well mattered just as much as – if not more than – money. I quickly made new friends and for the first time in ages I could honestly say I was having fun. However the money was pretty low compared to what I was used to earning and Christmas was looming so I decided to try and find a place to do additional work for the two-month run-up to Christmas. The first place I tried was out in Essex, and was recommended by a friend at the White Horse. I went there and thought it looked OK. It was decorated in gothic style and there was a pole but each girl only had to go on once during the night and there was no collection. It was all about the lap-dancing, and I mean proper lap-dancing. I was dancing for guys and they were complaining constantly, 'That was shit', 'Not worth a tenner'. I'd never had this in my life. Why was I doing so badly? Then I started to look around me.

This was dancing as I had never seen it before; this was proper bump and grind. Girls would be sat on a guy's lap, grinding back and forth on his dick in what is known as a 'dry fuck'. That was just the beginning. There were girls doing lesbian acts and actually licking each other's pussies. I didn't know what to think: someone told me that the lap-dancing scene had changed a lot since I was at Strings, due to more compe-tition and an influx of girls with extremely low standards. I expected some amount of closeness but not this. During the night, I saw one girl straddle a customer and let him finger her and lick her breasts; a girl put her hand into a guy's trousers, and a girl who just sat on a stool in front of a guy and masturbated. The two things that amazed me the most about this place, other than they were allowed to get away with this, was that half the girls were stunning: they could be earning a lot more to do a lot less somewhere else. Here they were giving everything away for eight quid a dance. (It actually cost a tenner a dance, but the club took two pounds off each girl.)

I was so stunned at what these girls were doing for so little money, even though I wouldn't have justified it for a lot more. I couldn't wait for my shift to end but I didn't want to walk out there and then as it would create a fuss. I just got on with it and tried to do some dances even though the punters were constantly saying 'closer' or 'I want to feel you'. The guys sickened me but if anything I danced even further away as I was so repulsed. With that night over and a swimsuit 'missing' out of my bag, I decided that place probably wasn't for me and I'd stick to the White Horse for now.

After that I didn't try anywhere else for a few weeks. I was really happy at the White Horse; the happiest I had ever been while dancing. There were fewer suits and more of the easygoing workmen type. The suits you got in there were also of a much better calibre. Because the place didn't offer private dancing, it would attract a different type of customer, so you were never hassled for sex or called a whore. The guys treated you like a star and were really complimentary. Not all of them, however. One busy Friday night I was walking to the toilet when a guy I had never laid eyes on before punched me in the stomach, kicked me in the shins and ran out of the door.

I was on the floor. The punch to the stomach hadn't really injured me as he'd got my side, so apart from being slightly winded I wasn't too badly hurt. He'd really messed up my shin, though. It was swelling up straight away. I was due to collect any second so I took a quick trip to the toilet, gladly accepted the brandy offered, put some stockings on to cover the marks and got on with my night. Long gone were the days when something like this would ruin my night or send me home crying. There was always someone to come to your aid, unlike Diamonds. I remember Sue, the owner, being so angry that the guy got away. She wasn't much older than the girls and had inherited the place from her parents. As much as she was a boss, she was also a friend. You'd see her on a Friday night on the floor with the girls, all of us tipsy, dancing around to some cheesy '80s music, like we were at a school disco. It was very different to any place I had worked before and, even today, is still one of my regular watering holes.

There were also regulars. Melissa had a guy who would put at least twenty pounds in her jug each time he visited and put a bottle of champagne on the bar for her. I had a regular who would visit me once a week, bringing me flowers and cookies. It was sweet and he was a lovely older guy, but it was everything I was trying to avoid after Strings and Diamonds. I didn't want to suck someone in and dump them. I didn't want to be in control of anyone's feelings, least of all this sweet old man. I decided to be nice to him and be a friend, which was obviously all he wanted.

Still worrying about earning so little money, I went for another audition. It was at a lap-dancing club that a friend of mine, Sam, worked at. The audition required me to do a dance for the manager. I thought this slightly unorthodox until I realised there was no pole at all (huge relief), but I hadn't done a private dance without a pole for over five years so I was slightly lost. I just kind of wiggled while disrobing, my legs trembling the whole time. It wasn't nerves; it was just that I was used to holding on to something and I was now realising how bad my balance had become. I passed my audition and started there a few days later. It was a proper lap-dancing club, nothing like the awful place I'd been to a few weeks before. It was like going back to the glamorous days of Strings with well-groomed, tanned girls in long evening dresses, dripping in diamantes. Hmm, competition would be fierce.

The club was beautiful inside, kind of like a trendy West End club meets old-fashioned gentleman's bar. It was set on five floors with the lap-dancing in the basement, the main bar on the ground floor, two upper floors for VIPs and, at the very top of the building, changing rooms. It was a pretty strenuous climb up to the top and as I panted my way up there was a girl I recognised from the White Horse. I opened my mouth to say 'Hi' but she just looked me up and down scowling and walked away. As I walked further into the changing room I couldn't help but hear the unmistakeable voice of my friend Sam. Thank God there was someone I knew. I joined her and got ready for my shift.

The dress code specified full-length evening dresses before 10pm but afterwards you could wear pretty much anything as long as you didn't show your bum. I had two main looks I favoured: the big-wavy-hair-and-sexy-swimsuit Bond-girl look. Or the corset-and-fishnets Moulin Rouge look. I hadn't worn an evening dress since I left Strings; to be honest I was glad to be rid of them but I dug one out. The 'no bum on show' rule meant I couldn't show off my fantastic array of swimwear. But I only planned to work for the Christmas period and only doing two shifts a week meant I could juggle the outfits I had.

I stood next to Sam and applied a heavy layer of war paint, donned my floor-length silver evening dress and made my way through the girls lavishing glitter all over their bodies. We trekked back down the four flights of stairs and when we got to the floor, she gave me the low-down and every bit of gossip I needed. Apparently the manager was an Oxford-educated guy who believed the strip scene was his true calling. He was a nice enough man, but a bit of a know-it-all. It was hard to spend too long in his company without feeling that he was condescending to you. He reminded me of many customers: insecure and constantly trying to boost his own ego.

The manager adored the girls and was constantly falling in love with them, but never got any further than a mild obsession. Sam had ended up in bed with him after the Christmas party but too much alcohol was consumed that night for anything more to happen and they never mentioned it after that. She told me he was nothing to worry about; he was really nice and would never straight-out hit on a girl. I don't think he was confident enough with women for that. The other manager had no qualms about hitting on anyone. I was quite surprised at his long line of conquests since his overpowering Mediterranean charm didn't do it for me. He was a real hard-arse though, and as soon as he realised I wasn't the kind of girl he could flirt with or be tactile with he took a dislike to me. He was always picking on the smallest things and pulling me up or talking down to me in front of customers. I'd been in the game too long to put up with his shit so I would always answer him back. This just aggravated him more so we clashed constantly.

He was one of the big factors in me starting to hate the club. He would speak to me in the most demeaning tone of voice and pull a face when he spoke to me like I was shit. I had to constantly bite my tongue around him otherwise it would have all blown up. One of the things I learned from Sam was that you had to hustle here, as there were a lot of big spenders. If you got them up to VIP then you'd make some real money, hundreds of pounds an hour in some cases. It had been years since I'd last hustled like that, but as much as everything had changed, the basics were still the same.

I did my first dance. It was lap-dancing; I saw some funny manoeuvres going on but I did what I was happy to do and no one complained. It was a good start even though the other girls were really getting close to the guys with their lap-dancing – although it was a far cry from what I had seen in the Essex club. I went up and down the stairs doing lap-dances for a while when I realised Sam was nowhere to be seen. A girl came up to me, introduced herself as Nadine and said Sam was in VIP and that she, Nadine, was to look after me. It was so typical of Sam to give me a babysitter to show me the ropes. We got a drink and had a chat and I was amazed that Sam had got a VIP already. Nadine explained it was one of her regulars: he came in all the time and she sat with him for four or five hours. I couldn't believe it. She was making a fortune, but it did make me wonder what the hell was going on for all that time. I asked Nadine what you needed to do to get the guys into VIP. 'Easy,' she said. We approached two guys stood at the bar and started a conversation with them.

'Hi, I'm Nadine, this is Ellie. So is it your first time here, guys?' These guys had a dance and left it at that, but she showed me the basic formula of how to work it.

Approach a guy and chat for five or ten minutes, then ask him if he wants a dance. When he's had a dance and you think he's really into you, ask him if he wants to take him up to the 'private' room. Now most of the guys know exactly what it is and frequent it often, so they know if they want it or not. Some guys might need the full chat-up. 'It's much quieter and more private upstairs, you can have me totally uninterrupted for an hour if you like. It's a lot more intimate, we can get to know each other a bit better and you can have me naked at any point.'

Sometimes you need to chat with the guys for a while but most guys go to VIP at some point in the night. The first time I went in, I didn't know what to expect so of course expected the worst. In the industry people always gossip about other clubs, and I'd heard rumours that girls would give blow jobs to the customers and do all sorts, but had spoken to Sam who laughed and dispelled my concerns. It was pretty quiet; there were three couples. I saw Sam, sat with her customer. She was naked, getting a back massage. Hmm, a bit intimate but not too bad. The next girl was doing a very intimate 'lap'-dance for her guy and she had certainly found his lap. In fact I wouldn't really call it a dance but it gave a new meaning to the word sit-down. The third couple were sat with a bottle of champagne, chatting. Not too bad. It was a bit too close for me but as long as I didn't have to do the really intimate stuff it would be fine.

I sat my customer down, did him a dance and we chatted for the whole hour, him swigging back the brandy, me sipping my same glass of champagne. The hour passed by so quickly and when the host approached us to tell us the hour was up, I thought, 'Shit, I didn't work hard enough, I've only done one dance, he's going to leave.' But he didn't. He stayed another hour, and then another. I couldn't believe it; it was my first night and I'd done three hours in VIP, just chatting and flirting. During the third hour, this big scary-looking girl with tattoos came up with her customer and sat right next to us. She started dancing and was so gross: she was putting her nipples into his mouth, touching herself and fake climaxing. There was no discretion here. My time was nearly up and the guy decided that was enough. Whether he'd just had enough or didn't like what he saw next to us I don't know, but I was pretty shocked because it was right in front of us. When I came back downstairs, I was feeling slightly different about the whole place. It just felt too full-on for me. I decided that as long as it didn't affect me too much, I'd keep trying.

By the end of that night, I'd earned great money. It seemed that most of the guys were regulars and there were quite a few high-flying bankers so there was certainly money to be made. The girl who was putting on the elaborate show in the VIP – also a new girl – was sacked the same night, so at least I knew the club didn't fuck around with girls who broke the rules. Within four or five shifts I was well rehearsed at how to work it. I returned to one of the ploys that I'd used at Strings: playing the part of a student.

My second night was really quiet, but almost immediately I had a guy make a beeline for me and ask me to join him. He told me he'd settle his bar bill downstairs and then take me to VIP. I excused myself for a moment to use the toilet and by the time I got back this horrible Northern girl was literally pulling him to the VIP area saying, 'You don't want her. Fake tits and fake ass, that's all she is,' as she pulled him from the room. So there went my sit-down and a lot of money. He was a regular so she knew he was a big spender. I was really pissed off but being the new girl couldn't really make a fuss. She was an awful drunk and really loudmouthed and vulgar so I knew from experience she was the kind of girl who would cause me trouble.

I'd persuaded Melissa to come and work there too. She was happy to add some extra shifts to her work at the White Horse. What made it even better was that we lived near each other so we made sure we worked the same shifts: at least if we were having a crappy shift we could stick together. On her first night, we approached guys together, which the guys loved. For some reason the whole sister thing is a huge turn-on for guys, I'm not sure why that is but we were making money and I've come across worse perversions. But still it was really hard. The club didn't get busy until about 10pm, and when you're there from 7pm, it gets kind of tiring. It was different in the early days at Strings when it was all new but now I seemed to have less tolerance for it all. At the same time, you really had to hustle. I'd always been blessed with not having to hustle and over the years I'd become less interested in it and now I found myself having to eye up guys and coax them. I found it all pretty tiring, probably because I wasn't really into it.

After about three weeks, both Melissa and I were struggling with the closeness of the dancing and the intimacy of the VIP as well as the hard hustle. We'd been out of the club scene for so long it was a sharp shock when we returned even though we'd gone to one of the nicer places. We would take turns to drive. On the nights you were drinking, it was so much easier to work, but sober you just saw the whole industry too clearly and now I found it repulsive. Both of us were wary of getting into a position where we could only work pissed.

We started to hate everything about it: the guys thinking they can buy you, the girls throwing themselves at the guys, having to sit in VIP for hours with a creep of a guy who smelt and was slobbering over you drunk. I began to feel disgusted with myself. The guys were making me feel ill. Maybe it wasn't so bad at Strings or I just don't remember, but a lot of the guys really smell. Thinking back, at Strings a lot of the punters weren't locals so they'd be staying in West End hotels, which meant they'd go back to their hotels before coming out. The guys here had been at work all day in a suit that hadn't seen the dry cleaners for a long time.

They'd been sweating all day, then gone out for drinks, so would stumble in around ten or eleven o'clock. So these men, who smelled of body odour/drink/food/cigarettes or a combination of all four, would be trying to fuck you. That's one of the reasons strippers wear so much perfume. But this wasn't just a superficial issue for me: it went much deeper.

It's as if everything had suddenly become all too clear. Most of the girls were totally pissed every night and there was no shortage of drugs flying around or guys asking you for sex. I started to remember the things I hated about Strings, and the club scene in general. In the VIP guys were constantly try to paw you or telling you what they'd like to do to you. It really fucked with your head. Sam was on coke every night and would have seven or more glasses of wine, too. Sometimes she'd even drive home after this: she was out of control. People started telling me she was a hooker. I just couldn't believe it, or maybe I didn't want to. It wasn't until I was talking to a punter one day – a young guy, decent-looking and a big hotshot banker in the City – and he told me that he had paid several of the girls for sex, one of them being Sam, that it sank in. Customers would tell you all sorts of rubbish, but still, she had definitely changed from the girl I knew. I heard rumours that she later got sacked.

One of the girls, Mandy, would be so pissed and all over the customers, kissing them and rubbing all over them. Management had banned her from drinking on the job but she sneaked her way around it. She was nearly forty, with two grown-up kids, and had got into stripping late in life. She'd been doing it for a good few years and all she really got from it was addictions. At the start of the night she'd be perfectly made up, funny, chatty and nice. By the end of the night, her makeup was smeared, her outfit would be hanging off and she'd be lying all over a customer, rubbing his crotch. (Mandy actually ended up marrying a customer and sorting herself out, which was lucky, very lucky. God knows what would have happened otherwise.) Meanwhile, Melissa also got married and her husband asked her to stop dancing. He hated it and in fairness to him, he'd put up with it for so long. Now he could no longer handle the woman he loved doing it. And so she left.

I had recently started dating someone. It was the first guy I'd dated after Greg and more importantly, the first man to really sweep me off my feet. I had no ideas about the future and was still very sceptical about men but I was ready and willing to give this one my all. He was not happy about the dancing situation at all, particularly the lap-dancing, so if this meant stopping dancing then so be it, for him as much as for me. This was all very foreign to me. I was having really strong feelings for the first time in my life, which went beyond stupid infatuation. Now, I was happy to do something for a man and that was to leave dancing. Maybe this was because I was looking for a way out but even so it was still out of character: it wasn't like me to let go and hand over control to another person. I carried on for about four more shifts without Melissa and then one night, I packed it in. It was mid-shift and there was this disgusting, lecherous guy, constantly saying he wanted to have sex with me and describing what he wanted to do while breathing his stagnant breath all over me. I felt physically sick. Then I got in another petty squabble with the manager and realised I didn't ever want to do this again. I changed, got my stuff and left.

It made me realise that I was truly done with the whole industry. I'd now pushed myself to a point where I hated it and everything about it. I no longer cared about earning more money. I had just bought my second flat, so I didn't need any more money. It was getting to the point of greed. I gave my notice at the White Horse and worked out the rest of my shifts. I was happy working there but I knew that it was time to leave everything; otherwise I would still be there when I was in my late thirties. From the day I started at Strings, I'd seen everything I didn't want to be. I was so close to becoming it on so many occasions, I had to leave now or I'd be stuck for ever. And this time I knew I would never return.

Chapter 24

Girl in bare feet

'So, where did it all go wrong, Ellouise?' Somebody actually asked me that once. I'm not sure it did go wrong. I've managed to make a very good living out of stripping without compromising my values. I've built up a property portfolio and, unlike a lot of girls, I got out of a business that holds many in its clutches. Anyhow, when people ask me that question what they really mean is, 'How does a nice girl like you end up in a place like this?' It was a question lots of punters asked, which made me smile, since they were also 'in a place like this'.

It's been over two years since I last stripped. The thought of going back and of being naked in public terrifies me, which is a good thing because I know I never will. People always ask me if I miss it, especially the money. I can honestly answer no, not even the money, because I can see the price I paid. Don't get me wrong – I have no regrets. Of course I've done things I'm not proud of and things have happened to me that I wish never had. But that's what life is and it's helped make me the person I am now.

I think I escaped relatively unscathed but the fact that I escaped at all is the biggest feat. I thank my lucky stars that I opened my eyes when I did. I constantly see or hear of girls in their late thirties and early forties, still stripping. They've been doing it for fifteen years and have nothing to show for it, no money, partner or friends, just designer handbags and a coke habit. When you're in that environment, it can be so seductive and all-encompassing, so you're blinded to what you've become or where your life is headed: the girls who can't physically do the job unless they're drunk or high; the greedy, money-obsessed girls who will go to any lengths for cash and will never have enough. Then there are the girls who enjoy it because it either satisfies a sordid sexual need, or they just can't live without the constant attention and adulation.

Being a stripper taught me much about insecurity, obsession, hatred, anger and greed. I discovered things I liked about myself and things I hated. The industry exposed me to great highs and lows, but in the end it made me realise how desperately I wanted a stable family life and children. It hasn't been easy though, not least the process of finding the real me. After quitting I went through a period of change. For the first time I allowed someone else, a man, to take control. A man who, as well as being well educated and smart, could say, 'Do you think you should do that?'

Quitting stripping also meant making huge lifestyle changes. I went from being a high-earning dancer to unemployed and pretty much unemployable (the longer I danced, the worse my CV looked) so I had to let a man support me, which believe me is still hard. I had some savings but these went on refurbishing my second flat. So my first major hurdle was allowing someone to help me. The second major change was in my confidence. Without the work clothes, makeup and flattery, I was just Ellouise, and I had to work out who that was. I was so used to putting on a sexy act and then suddenly that stopped and I went through a real crisis of confidence and identity.

It's taken the help of a loving and supportive partner to find my natural sensuality, without any acting or pretence. Over the past year especially I've found myself feeling more womanly, from the inside out, which is as it should be. I think if it wasn't for this support that I finally allowed myself to accept I may have started dancing again. He has stuck by me and moreover he's given me confidence to do new things. Perhaps the biggest indicator of my new-found trust is that I decided to buy a house with him. I freed up money from my first flat, which had gained in value considerably, and we put some money together to buy a place. This also freed up money to invest in a small run-down cottage in France for my mum's retirement.

It hasn't all been happy endings. Years of dancing in stupidly high heels mean that I now suffer painful hip problems: I've had surgery and will need more. Before, this would have set me back in my tracks, but it's amazing how much easier things are when there're two of you dealing with them. It's not all roses – relationships are hard work, bloody hard – but it's the first time I've actually been willing to work at one. Giving away some of my strength has made me gain even more, but a different type of strength, not a hard façade to protect myself, a genuine strength of character. I know I'm very fortunate as I still visit strip clubs – solely for the purpose of visiting my friends – and I realise how hard it is to leave. Every time I go to the White Horse, at least two people will ask me if I miss it or when I'm coming back. I just laugh and say I'm happy being broke. There's not a doubt left in my mind.

Of course it's not all about the girls; it's about the punters too. Where do you think *they* come from? Well, in my experience they come from everywhere, from all walks of life, and they're often the men you least expect. It might be your boyfriend, husband, brother, father, boss, colleague or the guy next door. Don't be so surprised: nothing in this world is what you think it is. You know those guys who argue loudly that they 'don't' or they just 'wouldn't'? Well, they do.

Next time you're on the tube or in the office, have a look at the man next to you and picture him in a strip club. Ask yourself, what kind of customer do you think he'd be? Is he the type to save me, the one who'll stalk me or the one wearing French knickers under his suit?